What others are saying about *THE RETIREMENT CRISIS . . . and the Real Estate Solution:*

I'm excited about Bob's book because people greatly underestimate the amount of money they're going to need to retire comfortably and real estate offers a vehicle to leverage the money they have.

Tom Karadza, Real Estate Investor, Author, Speaker

If you are 18 to 80 and want to take control of your life and your retirement, Bob's book is a must-read.

Raymond Aaron, #1 New York Times Bestselling Author
Double Your Income Doing What You Love;
and *Branding Small Business for Dummies*

Thanks to Bob's thorough book, you'll realize why investing in paper assets like mutual funds, stocks and bonds doesn't provide much money and has a whole world of risk that most people don't understand.

Erwin Zeto, Real Estate Investor, Speaker

Bob reveals how to tap into your hidden assets and maximize returns of your registered funds to achieve a more predictable retirement.

Daniel St-Jean, Real Estate Investor, Author, Speaker

If you have amassed some wealth and want to protect and grow your assets for a healthy retirement, then Bob's book is for you.

Victor Menasce, Real Estate Investor, Author, Speaker

Real estate is a fantastic wealth creator that can help you retire more comfortably and Bob introduces opportunities that most people don't even know about it.

Julie Broad, Real Estate Investor, Author, Speaker

You will want to take action and gain control of your finances through real estate for a rewarding retirement after reading Bob's information-packed and fun book.

Robert Allen, #1 New York Times Bestselling Author
Creating Wealth; Nothing Down; Multiple Streams of Income;
and *The One Minute Millionaire*

THE RETIREMENT CRISIS

...and the Real Estate

Solution

THE RETIREMENT CRISIS . . . and the Real Estate Solution

ISBN 978-1-7727702-5-4

Dog and Pony Productions Inc.
51 Rosebery Place
St. Thomas, Ontario, Canada N5R 2H9

Credits:
Editing, Anna Mae Fipke, Spirit Seekers Publishing
Front cover and book design, Dominique Petersen,
www.AuthorConsultants.org

Printed in Canada

This book is dedicated to my Mother for her passion,
her enduring strength and her sense of travel and adventure;

and to my Father for his wit, his warmth and empathy
toward others, and his knowledge and loving regard for nature.

ACKNOWLEDGEMENTS

I am in gratitude for the many people who made this book possible. They mentored and encouraged me in so many ways, especially when I had no idea that the research and writing would take over two years to complete and that I would end up doing almost a complete rewrite.

I am grateful every day for my wonderful wife, Gail, who inspires me with her own creativity and writing abilities. She has written several books and exudes 'art from the heart'. Her patience and support has been invaluable.

I would also like to extend my sincere thanks and heartfelt appreciation to:

Raymond Aaron, real estate investor, educator, author and mentor who inspires me every month when I listen to his interviews with famous and influential people. His enthusiasm and passion is contagious, and has been instrumental in leading me through the steps to writing and marketing my book.

Robert Allen, author, educator and real estate investor, for his support and unique story-telling style; it was his inspiration and suggestion that I rewrite my book and relay the information as a story. Thank you, Robert!

Tom Karadza, real estate investor, educator and author, for his inspiration and mentoring. His weekly newsletters, monthly CD's, publications and live presentations by Tom and his brother, Nik, are very informative and inspiring.

Daniel St-Jean, real estate investor, author and mentor, for his time, support and willingness to share his ideas and strategies regarding the rent-to-own, joint ventures, and taking action sections of my book.

David Chilton, author of *The Wealthy Barber,* for his words of encouragement and powerful example of educating through story telling.

Anna Mae Fipke, my editor, who helped me to look at things differently and supported my race to the finish line.

Dominique Petersen, who amazed me with the front cover design, and formatted the book to press-ready stage under a tight timeline.

Ann-Marie Cheung, my webmaster, for her creativity and assistance with my website and online connections.

My mentors in real estate and joint ventures: Victor Menasce, Julie Broad, Don Campbell, Erwin Zeto, Mark Greenidge and Rhonda Landgren.

And to the many people that took the time to comment on my drafts, make title suggestions and keep me motivated: Gail McNaughton, Allison Burney, Jason Clements, Tim Schnurr, Dave Ventura, Allan Weatherall and Brenda Smallman.

TABLE OF CONTENTS

FOREWORD

- Do you ever wonder what your life could be like with better investment choices?
- Are you worried that you didn't start saving soon enough?
- Do you know how much you need to retire?
- Are you running around with no time to plan or execute a retirement strategy?
- Do you worry about not having enough for retirement?

If you answered yes to any of these questions, you need to read this book! You may be in a retirement crisis.

Find out answers to your critical retirement questions:

1. How much do I save?
2. How do I invest?
3. How do I withdraw?

Are you eighteen to eighty, Canadian or American, and wanting to take control of your life and your retirement? Then *The Retirement Crisis* is a must-read. You will be there with nine people of all ages that Jonquil, a young reporter, organized through Meetup.com, and you will learn strategies to achieve your retirement dreams.

This enticing story will remind you of David Chilton's classic, *The Wealthy Barber,* as you benefit from the wisdom that Bob shares through Jonquil.

You will find this book an eye-opener and life-changer! You will not have to reinvent the wheel, or get burned by trial and error. You just have to follow the path laid out for you in the pages of this book.

Discover how to maximize your return on time—your scarcest resource. You can make more money and you can build more equity, but you cannot make more time!

Learn how you can make money with real estate:

1. Increase equity with mortgage repayment
2. Positive cash flow
3. Appreciation

Did you know that real estate is the common thread among millionaires and was my ticket to financial success? Did you know that one of the best investors of our time, Warren Buffet, once said, "The best time to invest in real estate was thirty years ago, the next best time is today!"

You will learn "The Retirement Secret" and how to tap into your hidden assets to maximize your RRSP returns and achieve a more predictable retirement. Get started even if you have no time, no cash and no knowledge.

Pay close attention to what you read in this book. Enjoy the story, and above all else, take action and put the ideas to use for you and your family.

May you be inspired to go out and achieve your dreams and enjoy a retirement that you plan for and deserve!

Sincerely,
Raymond Aaron

Chapter 1:

WHAT IS RETIREMENT?

Jonquil was pleased. All nine members of the Meetup.com group she had organized were present for their first ever 'in person' meeting. As soon as they were all settled in, she opened the meeting with the question, "What is retirement? What does retirement look like to you? I would like each of you to tell the group your name, age range, occupation, background, why you are here and what your image of retirement is."

Each member presented their own unique perception of what 'retirement' meant to them. Since this was the first time they had met in person, some were more eager to share than others.

Jenny envisioned trekking that spiritual mountain that was so elusive all her life. She never had the money or the time to travel, especially on a month-long journey halfway around the world. She was thirty-seven years old and worked as a nurse in the local hospital. Her marriage had ended in a difficult divorce that left her with little savings and no alimony.

Still in his forties, Jordan planned to follow his passion for the outdoors and work part-time leading outdoor adventure trips. Currently, he worked long hours as the owner of a family dental practice. On weekends, he could hardly wait to escape to nature with his family. They were active cyclists and campers in the summer and headed to the ski hills in the winter.

Jackie, in her early fifties, wanted to spend time with her grandchildren. She had taught school most of her life and really enjoyed children. During her summers off, she would happily babysit for her three children who lived nearby, and looked forward to doing more of the same.

Jeff was sixty-six and dreamed of sitting on a beach in a warm climate. He was still driving his own transport truck and hated winter more and more as he got older. Long haul trips did not appeal to him, but he had to keep working. His investments had been a roller-coaster. He had lived a good life and now had very little saved for retirement.

Judit loved people and worked as a salesperson at a local retail store. She had worked hard all her life and had saved since she was a teenager. She prided herself on being very thrifty; she and her husband did not eat out or travel. They had raised five children and, now in their forties, were enjoying their family home. They planned to retire there and tend to their gardens.

Jonathan was an entrepreneur. He had dabbled in several businesses and investments. Some made money and others had not. Cruising into his late fifties, his retirement dream was freedom to do what he wanted, when he wanted, whether it was traveling to sporting events around the world, working a part-time business, or enjoying a warm winter retreat. He knew that he needed to focus and develop a plan to achieve his desire for freedom in retirement.

Jay, the youngest in the room, seemed quiet and shy. At twenty-six, he was single and had his own online business. A bright, forward thinker, he wanted to learn from the trials and errors of the older members of the group. He enjoyed travel, and his dream for when he retired was to travel farther and longer with no specific schedule.

Jeremy was reluctant to say anything. His desk job as a manager for a large manufacturer meant long hours on the computer. He had not kept up any exercise program and was out of shape. His finances were also out of shape, since he and his wife would eat out almost every night. They had no budget, or plan for retirement. As one of the older members of the group, he would not reveal his age, but he did allude to the fact that he might never be able to retire.

Jonquil was the outgoing 'flower' of the group. As a reporter in her thirties, she was researching and writing a story on retirement. With her skill using social media, she had reached out to people of all ages and backgrounds to recruit this diverse group. She eventually wanted to build a foundation to help disadvantaged young people start their own businesses, so they would be able to retire successfully.

After everyone had offered their response, Jonquil told the group that there are probably as many views about retirement as there are people on the planet. She agreed that retirement could encompass the positives, like sitting on a beach in a warm climate, trekking that elusive spiritual mountain, spending time with your grandchildren, building a foundation to support young people, or working part-time in a business you are passionate about. But she also warned that the not-so-positive realities also existed, such as no retirement, having to work until the day you die, living in poverty, or spending your last days in a subsidized retirement facility.

Jonquil then made a powerful statement:

> *'The truth is that the positive images may not happen, but the negative images do not have to be your reality!'*

RETIREMENT DEFINITION

Jonquil went on to read the Wikipedia definition of retirement:

> *Retirement is the point where a person stops employment completely. A person may also semi-retire by reducing work hours.*

Many people choose to retire when they are eligible for private or public pension benefits. Some are forced to retire when physical conditions no longer allow them to work because of illness or accident, or as a result of legislation concerning their position. In most countries, the idea of retirement is of recent origin, being introduced during the late 19th and early 20th centuries. Previously, low life expectancy and the absence of pension arrangements meant that most workers continued to work until death. Germany was the first country to introduce retirement, in 1889.

Today, most developed countries have systems to provide pensions on retirement in old age, which may be sponsored by employers and/or the government. In many poorer countries, support for the old is still mainly provided through the family. Now, retirement with a pension is considered a right of the worker. In many Western countries this right is mentioned in national constitutions.

A person may retire at whatever age they please. However, a country's tax laws and/or government old age pension rules usually mean that a certain age is thought of as the 'standard' retirement age. This varies from country to country, but it is generally between fifty and seventy.

THE HEALTH FACTOR AND THE WEALTH FACTOR

Jonquil summarized the two key factors that affect all retirement decisions—health and wealth.

How healthy are you?
This affects longevity (how long you will live) and lifestyle (how active you can be).

How wealthy are you?
This also affects longevity and lifestyle (how long can you afford

to live your preferred lifestyle). In general, people are living longer and their savings may not support their longer life span.

The rising cost of living during retirement is a serious concern to many older adults. The cost of health care in retirement is huge, because people tend to be ill more frequently in later life. Most countries provide universal health insurance coverage for seniors, although many people retire before their eligibility at age sixty-five.

Early retirement can be at any age, but is generally before the age or tenure needed for eligibility for support from government or employer-provided sources. Early retirees rely on their own savings and investments to be initially self-supporting until they start receiving external support.

Accepting termination of employment before retirement age, which includes a monetary inducement, is becoming more common as part of an employer's labour force rationalization.

Individuals in poor health usually retire earlier than those in better health. In general, declining health over time, as well as the onset of new health conditions, is related to earlier retirement.

Jonquil asked the group, "When do you want to retire?" and listened to their responses. The younger people wanted to retire in their fifties and sixties. Some wanted to continue working part-time, and others could not see themselves ever completely retiring.

Jackie had done some homework and made these revelations. Several factors affect people's retirement decisions. Government pensions clearly play an important role. People are much more likely to retire at the early and normal retirement ages of the public pension system (ages 60 and 65 in Canada, or 62 and 65 in the U.S.). Individuals respond significantly to financial incentives relating to retirement (e.g. Social Security in the U.S. and Canada Pension Plan (CPP) and Old Age Security (OAS) in Canada).

Greater wealth tends to lead to earlier retirement, since wealthier individuals can essentially 'purchase' additional leisure.

Income after retirement can come from government pensions, occupational pensions, private savings and investments, inheritances and social benefits. The heavy financial weight of provision for pensions on a government's budget is the reason for political debates about the retirement age and some governments are interested in a later retirement age for economic reasons.

Jonathan, speaking from experience, told how the financial crisis that began in 2007 is affecting retirement decisions. Fewer people will retire, since their savings have been depleted. Many who retire will continue to work, but not in the career they had for the majority of their life. Job openings will increase in the next five years, due to retirements of the baby boomer generation.

Jonquil jumped in with her findings that many people are married when they reach retirement age, so their spouse's employment status may affect their decision to retire. On average, in Canada and the U.S., husbands are three years older than their wives, and spouses often coordinate their retirement decisions. Thus, men are more likely to retire if their wives are also retired; more so than if their wives are still in the labour force. This works the other way as well, Jonquil was quick to point out.

LIFE AFTER RETIREMENT

Jonquil continued with research that said:

> *Retirement may coincide with important life changes. You may move to a new location, for example a retirement community, and have less frequent contact with your friends and adopt a new lifestyle.*

Often retirees volunteer for charities and other community organizations. Travel is a common marker of retirement and, for some, becomes a way of life. Some retired people even choose to live in warmer climates, known as retirement migration.

There are six lifestyle choices as Americans and Canadians age:

1. Continuing to work full-time.
2. Continuing to work part-time.
3. Retiring from work and becoming engaged in a variety of leisure activities.
4. Retiring from work and becoming involved in a variety of recreational and leisure activities.
5. Retiring from work and later returning to work part-time.
6. Retiring from work and later returning to work full-time.

Jonquil noted from these lifestyle definitions that four of the six involve working! Canada and the U.S. are facing an important demographic shift since the baby boomer generation is now at retirement age. This poses two challenges:

i) will there be a sufficient number of skilled workers in the work force, and
ii) will the current pension programs be sufficient to support the growing number of retired people.

Jenny noted that retirees are often called upon to care for grandchildren and, occasionally, aged parents. For many, it gives them more time to devote to a hobby or sport. On the other hand, many retirees feel restless and suffer from depression as a result of their new situation. Although it is not scientifically possible to directly show that retirement either causes or contributes to depression, the newly retired are one of the most vulnerable societal groups when it comes to depression. This is most likely due to the combination of increasing age and deteriorating health status.

Studies have shown that healthy elderly and retired people are as happy, or happier, and have an equal quality of life as they age, as compared to younger employed adults. Therefore, retirement in and of itself, is not likely to contribute to the development of depression.

Jenny concluded that many people in their later years, due to deteriorating health, will require assistance, sometimes with expensive treatments provided in a nursing home. Those who need care, but are not in need of constant assistance, may choose to live in a retirement home.

As the meeting came to a close, Jonquil thanked everyone for their valuable contributions. She then asked for feedback on future meetings. "How often do you think we should get together, and where and when would be best for everyone?"

Jonathan, Jenny and Jordan all liked the time and location that Jonquil had arranged for their initial meeting. They suggested that the group meet weekly, same time, same place.

Everyone agreed. They knew that there was much to discover and plan for their own retirement. The group liked the idea that there were a variety of ages, backgrounds, education, experience, retirement knowledge and occupations represented. They were excited to continue their learning through research and discussion.

Jonquil ended the meeting by saying, "Next week we'll talk about the numbers—how much we need and key considerations. Since there is Wi-Fi here, we'll go online and view some websites and retirement calculators. Please bring your smartphone, tablet or laptop so you can bookmark some websites for future reference. See you next week!"

Chapter 2:

HOW MUCH DO YOU NEED?

Jonquil used her iPad to emphasize her next key points. "First of all," she said, "there are three important questions that you must consider when it comes to retirement:

1. How much do you need to save for retirement?
2. How do you invest that money?
3. How do you withdraw that money so you don't outlive your assets?"

She had spent many hours trying to answer the first question by talking to retirement 'specialists' and researching online retirement calculators to determine the 'ideal' number. To her surprise and disappointment, there was no magic formula, equation, or ideal number that offered an answer; mainly because everyone has different goals, needs and circumstances that require different actions.

Jonquil found a summer 2011 survey by the Canadian Payroll Association, where forty per cent of respondents said they would likely now retire later than they had originally planned. The main reason stated by forty percent of those people was they had not saved enough for retirement. Sixty per cent of respondents said they were trying to be better savers.

In her research, Jonquil heard many grim stories of senior citizens who could not afford to eat well, or travel, or live in their preferred retirement home. In general, they could not enjoy life the way they had expected to. Others said, "This won't happen to me," but then the self-doubts start to creep in.

Some experts estimate that you will need to accumulate $800,000 before you can afford to retire. That is when people spring into panic mode and check out the online retirement calculators.

Jonquil cautioned that before jumping onto a retirement calculator, you need to do some soul-searching.

RETIREMENT WORKSHEET

Realizing everyone's uniqueness, Jonquil devised a simple way to calculate savings (past actions) and income (circumstances) as credits (+), and needs (health and welfare) and wants (goals) as debits (-). The concept was simple, but would require individual soul-searching and discussion with a spouse or partner.

Jonquil drew one line down the centre of a lined piece of paper creating two columns and labelled them 'credits' (+) and 'debits' (-). She asked each of the group members to do the same and label their sheet, "My Retirement Worksheet" (see page 11). This was going to be a key part of their homework for the next couple of months.

Jonquil had already talked about health and wealth as key factors in retirement planning. In her research, she realized that they are on opposite sides of the equation.

Wealth is a credit resulting from past actions, and actions regarding present and future circumstances. These include previous savings (stocks, bonds, GICs, real estate, precious metals), current income (salary, commission, rent, disability pension), current savings (stocks, bonds, GICs, real estate, precious metals), projected growth (interest, dividends, capital gains) future income (salary, commission, rent, government pension, company pension), future savings (regular and lump sum contributions) and ultimate savings upon retirement (total net worth = assets – liabilities).

MY RETIREMENT WORKSHEET	
Credits (+)	**Debits (-)**

Each of the items in brackets, and any other appropriate items, would occupy a specific line on the retirement worksheet.

Savings at retirement is the big number that everything else will be subtracted from. Future income and growth after retirement will help to prolong one's ability to maintain their preferred standard of living.

Health is a debit, and a catch 22! Poor health may require more monthly withdrawals to pay for health care. Good health may prolong life and the necessity for increased retirement savings. That was surprising to some in the group.

Jordan was proud of his health and fitness level. He suddenly realized that, because of his good health and fitness habits, he would probably live longer and would require more retirement savings to maintain his lifestyle. His 'number' needed to be bigger.

Jeremy was in deep contemplation, as he realized that he had some choices to make. He could remain in poor shape and pay for it through increased health care costs and a reduced standard of living. Or he could choose to become more health conscious, get some exercise, start eating healthy foods and get sufficient sleep which, in turn, would improve his retirement lifestyle and his longevity. Either choice would impact his 'number'.

Jonquil brought the group back to the debit side by discussing needs and wants. 'Needs' pertain to the basics of living—including food, shelter, clothing, health care and some basic entertainment or hobby.

'Wants' refer to lifestyle preferences—personal goals, pets, relationships, entertainment and hobbies. This includes your wish list or 'bucket list' of things you want to do, see, be or accomplish in this lifetime. These wants all draw on and reduce your savings.

Jenny jumped in and relayed her story about her goals and lifestyle preferences not matching with her husband's goals and lifestyle preferences. The older they got, the more divergent they became. "That was part of the reason that we could not continue living together," she stated.

Jackie pointed out that if you have a spouse or partner, their lifestyle preferences and goals must be considered to ensure a happy retirement. That may lead to long, but important discussions. Her son had also moved back home when he lost his job and had not found another job in almost a year. She knew that would delay retirement for herself and her husband.

Jonathan underscored the importance of tolerance and understanding in a relationship by saying, "Happy wife/partner . . . happy life . . . and retirement!" (See the "Spouse/Partner Retirement Worksheet" on page 14.)

Jonquil then drew three lines on another piece of paper that created four columns, two each for an individual and their spouse or partner. "As you can see," she stated, "having a partner can be more complicated, but also more rewarding as you can add your credits to their credits and hopefully economize on the debits." (See "My Retirement and My Spouse/Partner Retirement Worksheet" on page 15.)

She suggested that each group member with a spouse or partner use a two-column worksheet to map out their own credits and debits; then work with their partner to complete their list of credits and debits. Once both partners have completed their own worksheets, combine the information on a four-column worksheet, then work together to determine how to maximize the credit side and economize with the debits.

SPOUSE/PARTNER RETIREMENT WORKSHEET	
Credits (+)	**Debits (-)**

MY RETIREMENT AND MY SPOUSE/PARTNER RETIREMENT WORKSHEET			
My Credits (+)	**My Debits (-)**	**Partner Credits (+)**	**Partner Debits (-)**

WILL I OUTLAST MY SAVINGS?

Jonquil shared some specific research that certainly got everyone's attention. She said that many people have their savings in the stock market with mutual funds, stocks and bonds.

While conventional wisdom says that you can retire and take seven per cent or more out of a portfolio year after year, this would not have worked very often in the past. Many assumptions that are based on long-term average investment returns can be meaningless when based on making periodic inflation-adjusted withdrawals from retirement savings.

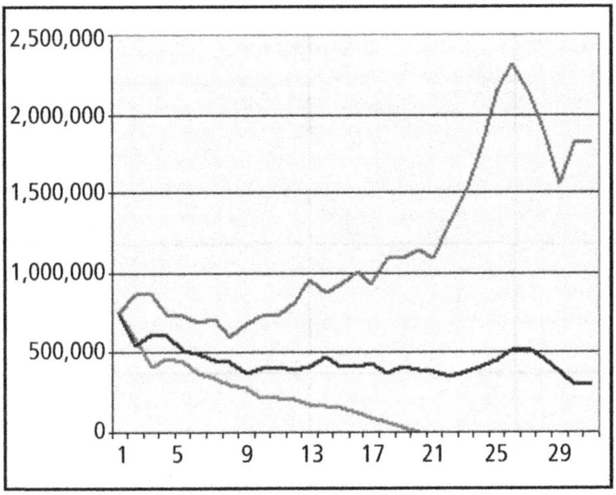

Jonquil displayed the U.S. chart above that showed the year-to-year portfolio balances after taking $35,000 (and adjusting for inflation) from a $750,000 portfolio every year for thirty years, starting in 1973 (bottom line), 1974 (middle line), or 1975 (top line).

Jordan had his iPad and wanted to know the URL so he could reference the article. Jonquil gave the link to her website: **theretirementcrisis.com** and asked the group to find the URL under **Online Tool #1**. Jordan, and others, pulled it up right away and followed along.

The article explained that while the overall market conditions and inflation affected all three investors about the same (since all three experienced exactly the same conditions between 1975 and 2003), the chance of making the funds last for thirty years depended heavily on what happened to the stock market in the first few years.

Those thinking of early retirement will want to know if they have enough saved up to survive possible bear markets, such as the one that would cause the hypothetical 1973 retiree's fund to be exhausted after only twenty years. Jonquil explained that a 'bear market' is when stock prices are falling and that encourages selling.

The history of the U.S. stock market shows that an investor would need to live on about four per cent of the initial portfolio per year to ensure that the portfolio is not depleted before the end of their retirement.

The four per cent figure does not assume any pension, or change in spending levels, throughout retirement. This allows for increasing the withdrawals with inflation to maintain a consistent spending ability throughout retirement, and to continue making withdrawals even in dramatic and prolonged bear markets.

Jonquil pointed out that this real world example using the U.S. stock market is generally applicable to stock markets in other countries, especially Canada, where the markets are often (although not always) in synch.

This example demonstrates the risks involved when investing and relying only on the stock market for your savings, building your retirement nest egg, then withdrawing your savings under differing market conditions. The greater the volatility experienced in the market, the greater the risk of running out of money. She warned that this is especially true in today's wildly fluctuating markets.

MANUAL CALCULATION

For Jay and other analytical types, Jonquil found a manual calculation that could be done on a computer spreadsheet. It assumes that interest, after expenses, taxes and inflation is zero.

Assume that in real terms (after-inflation), your salary never changes during your w years of working life. During your p years of pension, you have a living standard which costs a replacement ratio R times as much as your living standard in your working life. Your working life living standard is your salary less the proportion of salary Z that you need to save. Calculations are per unit salary, e.g. assume salary = 1.

Then after w years work, retirement age accumulated savings = wZ. To pay for pension for p years, necessary savings at retirement = $Rp(1\text{-}Z)$

Equate these: $wZ = Rp(1\text{-}Z)$ and solve to give $Z = Rp \,/\, (w + Rp)$. For example, if $w = 35$, $p = 30$ and $R = 0.65$ we find that we need to save a proportion $Z = 35.78$ per cent of our salary.

ONLINE RETIREMENT CALCULATORS

For most of the group, an online retirement calculator sounded much more appealing!

Jonquil used a Google search for 'retirement calculator' that produced a staggering 32,100,000 results. It was immediately apparent that not all calculators are created equal. This brought up more questions: Which calculators should you rely on? What is the best way to use them?

"FIRECalc is a different kind of retirement calculator; it's actually the one we utilized for the previous example," Jonquil stated. "You can find it on my website: **theretirementcrisis.com** under **Online Tool #2**. This calculator uses historical U.S. stock market modeling, and adds provisions for incorporating pensions, other retirement income and any changes in spending that may occur during the course of your retirement. My website offers specific tabs for other income and spending, pre-retirement, spending models, current portfolio status, portfolio changes, as well as a tab to investigate other options for your retirement plan.

"If you are considering early retirement in the U.S., there is a ten per cent IRS (Internal Revenue Service) penalty on withdrawals from a retirement plan such as a 401(k) or a traditional IRA (Individual Retirement Account) when retiring prior to age 59.5. Exceptions apply under certain circumstances. To avoid this ten per cent penalty, an individual should consult a lawyer about the use of IRS rule 72 T that must be applied for through the IRS.

"If the calculator you have selected asks about your Roth IRA or 401(k) plan, you are using a U.S. calculator." Jonquil warned that Canadians need to make sure they are using a calculator designed for Canadian investors.

She found several online retirement calculators for Canada and selected those that were not affiliated with banks or other financial institutions. She showed the group three pre-retirement calculators and gave an overview for each. Jonquil would not make any recommendations, as she knew that everyone's circumstances and preferences were different.

The Canadian Government Retirement Income Calculator can be found at **theretirementcrisis.com, Online Tool #3**. This link from the Canadian government will provide retirement income information including the Old Age Security (OAS) pension and Canada Pension Plan (CPP) retirement benefits. You work through a series of modules in order to estimate your retirement income from various sources and compare them to your income goal. You can also see the impact of changes in your savings.

Another calculator that helps you plan your cash flow in retirement and estimate how long your money will last is: Get Smarter about Money—Retirement Cash Flow Calculator at **theretirementcrisis.com, Online Tool #4**.

A key benefit to this site is the ability to see the impact of changes in external factors (investment return, inflation) and personal choices (lifestyle decisions, spending) on your cash flow.

A new software program was described in 'MoneySense'. Have a look at **theretirementcrisis.com, Online Tool #5**. It is an elaborate financial projection calculator that allows you to enter the details of your particular situation, such as your age, your salary and when you hope to kick off your golden years. It then calculates how much you need to save each year, what your nest egg will be worth and how much you will need to live on. It automatically factors in your Canada Pension Plan and Old Age Security payments, and also accounts for mortgage payments, your spouse's income, taxes and other factors.

Jonquil found a specific post-retirement calculator from RetirementAdvisor.ca to answer this question for Canadians: "Will I have enough money?" Check out **Online Tool #6** at **theretirementcrisis.com**. This post-retirement calculator is designed for people who are considering retiring soon, or for those who have already retired. It will help them determine a 'ballpark' estimate of how much retirement income they may receive. By inputting your personal and financial information, you can compute your estimated total retirement income, along with a detailed projection of your assets during retirement. It is designed to use your financial resources in such a manner as to provide you with as consistent a retirement income estimate as possible over your entire retirement period.

RETIREMENT CALCULATOR TIPS AND CAUTIONS

Jonquil then provided a few tips and cautions that she had learned to guide everyone through this very crowded field. Some of these tips were specifically for Canadians.

1. Be realistic in your projections.

"This is the most important advice that retirement consultants gave me for retirement calculators," said Jonquil. Many calculators will ask you to enter the performance you expect from your investments, both before and after retirement. Be conservative!

Many investors expect their investments to earn double-digit returns, year after year. That often happened in the 1980's and 1990's, but not these days. Most pros and the better calculators now recommend a more conservative four to five per cent after fees, based on the current state of very low interest rates and volatile market returns.

When asked to estimate the future average annual inflation rate, aim high. Inflation is negligible now, but has historically been two and a half to three per cent.

A Bank of Canada Inflation Calculator at **theretirementcrisis.com, Online Tool #7** provides an eye-opening, long-term perspective on the CPI (Consumer Price Index) and shows how escalating prices can devastate purchasing power over time.

2. Assume you will live to be ninety.

Many websites offer life-expectancy calculators that are fun to fill out, but can spit out wildly varying results depending on the questions being asked. Jonquil warned that whatever the answer, you need to understand what it means.

Mortality tables provide the median life expectancy. That means that half of all men who are now forty will live beyond seventy-eight. Half will not make it to that age. Be optimistic and assume you will make it to ninety. Great news if it happens, but it does mean you will need to save more.

3. Assume you will live a busy, active (more expensive) retirement.

After the group's initial discussion on what retirement meant to each of them, they knew that retirement is more than just sitting in a rocking chair and sipping tea. Today's seniors are the healthiest, most active over sixty-five set ever.

Leisure time costs money . . . golf, travel, a second home, are all expensive propositions.

When your retirement calculator asks what percentage of your income (in today's dollars) you hope to retire with, ask yourself how much lower your expenses will be in retirement.

Many calculators suggest you enter a retirement income goal that is seventy per cent of your pre-retirement income. The experts told Jonquil that some people may be able to get by with as little as fifty per cent. You will not be contributing to your savings or RRSP any more, the kids will be on their own, you will be in a lower tax bracket and your home will likely be paid off. If you are not in that camp, you had better raise your retirement income assumptions.

4. Be aware of the questions the calculator is not asking.
Jonquil had tried many calculators and realized that some do not ask important questions like the current value of RRSPs, company pension plans or investments made outside RRSPs. She recommends calculators such as RetirementAdvisor.ca (in the previous section) that takes into account newer financial opportunities like the tax-free savings account (TFSA).

Some calculators did not adequately take into account government programs like the Canada Pension Plan and Old Age Security. Other calculators did not provide the flexibility to figure out the difference between taking your CPP retirement pension early at age sixty, or waiting until age seventy. Sixty-five is the standard starting age.

Jonquil told the group not to believe people who tell you not to count on the Canada Pension Plan for any retirement benefits. In July 2009, just a few months after the stock market crash, Canada's chief actuary said the CPP is sustainable for the next seventy-five years. "The CPP," she said, "will be around when all of us in this room retire—even you Jay!"

5. The longer the questionnaire, the better.
Jonquil found out that some calculators ask just three or four questions and are quick to fill out, but they will not give you a complete picture. Other calculators warn that it will take thirty minutes to use them. Great! The more questions they ask of you, the better.

The Canadian Government Retirement Income Calculator (in the previous section) is a gold standard in the field. Its detail about the various income security programs cannot be beat. If you have a pension plan at work, it has a good list of pension-related questions to ask your employer.

6. Be aware of a retirement calculator's limitations.
Another key tip that Jonquil learned and passed on to the group was that retirement calculators are just interactive computer programs. They cannot tell you what to invest in, or determine your risk profile. They cannot offer tax advice or suggest ways of income-splitting with a spouse. They cannot advise on whether you should take your CPP at age sixty or wait until sixty-five or seventy.

These are areas where professional financial planning advice can come in handy. Advocis, the Financial Advisors Association of Canada, has some questions you should ask anyone who wants to manage your finances. Check them out at **theretirementcrisis.com, Online Tool #8**.

7. Do not confuse the message with the messenger.
Jonquil asked everyone to pay special attention to this cautionary tip. If a calculator suggests that the best way to make up your projected gap in retirement savings is to buy specific mutual funds (Bank A's mutual funds on Bank A's calculator), the warning bells should be sounding!

Getting unbiased advice about retirement is critical. Independent financial advice may steer you in directions that would be far more appropriate for your situation than Bank A's mutual funds. There are plenty of ways to save for retirement, both inside and outside an RRSP.

Jonquil told the group they would be learning a lot about enhancing their awareness regarding recommendations and motives—understanding the message and the messenger—at their next meeting.

8. Take action on the calculator's answers.

Jonquil's last tip was very profound. Calculators can be great motivators, but they can only do so much. If the calculator finds that you are more likely to face a hand-to-mouth retirement than the comfortable retirement you were hoping for, then you (and only you) will have to do something about it.

One thing retirement calculators all show, is that time can be a real enemy. Delaying retirement saving until you are sixty is asking for trouble. Start saving when you are twenty-five, and suddenly your job becomes a lot easier. Consult a pro, buy and read a retirement planning book . . . just do something!

Jonquil had a special meeting planned for the group at the end of their weekly sessions on taking action.

She summarized the day's meeting, noting that by conscientiously using a retirement worksheet and inputting detailed information into a good retirement calculator, and following the tips above, most people should be able to answer questions one and three below:

1. How much do you need to save for retirement?
2. How do you invest that money?
3. How do you withdraw that money so you do not outlive your assets?

The group would spend most of the following weeks learning how to answer question two: "How do you invest that money?"

Jonquil confirmed that the group would meet at the same place, same time next week and gave them some homework to begin to answer question two.

"Watch the PBS Frontline television special, 'The Retirement Gamble' at **theretirementcrisis.com, Online Tool #9**. Take notes and be prepared for more discussion!"

Chapter 3:

WHAT YOU WERE NOT TAUGHT IN SCHOOL

"How many of you watched the Frontline TV special from PBS—The Retirement Gamble—online this week?" Jonquil asked. She watched with surprise as everyone in the group raised their hand. "Wow!" she said. "You really are serious about wanting to figure out a 'retirement solution!' Perhaps, I'll make my own documentary about 'The Retirement Solution', or write a book after I publish my story for the media."

She continued, "Let's review the key points in the documentary. Somebody start us off."

Jonquil got another surprise when Jeremy jumped in first. "America is facing a retirement crisis," he said. "Half say they can't afford to save for retirement and one third have next to no savings at all."

Jeremy told the group that the documentary really hit him hard. He was an American who had transferred to a manufacturing plant in Canada and retained his U.S. citizenship. He and his wife lost most of what little savings they had in the stock market. They had relatives and friends in the U.S. that lost their homes and businesses with the housing crisis in 2008 and the downturn in the economy, so he could empathize with the people in the video.

Jeremy had noted each person's name, occupation and age in the video:
Robert, economist, age 31
Crystal, teacher, age 32
Mark, unemployed sales manager, age 54
Laura, office manager, age 48
Bob, semi-retired former teacher, age 67
Martin, correspondent, age 64

"Martin," Jeremy pointed out, "produced the documentary and narrated much of it. He started saving for his retirement in his late twenties, divorced, suffered the crash of 2008, plans on working to age seventy, then part-time to seventy-five. He realized that a critical element to retirement is having enough return on your savings but (mutual fund) fees really hinder those returns. Martin was told that you need ten to twelve times pay to retire."

Jonquil jumped in to alleviate any of the groups concerns that the documentary was not relevant for Canadians. "In Canada, as you will find out later," she said, "mutual fund fees are actually higher and, therefore, more devastating than they are in the States. So the video is definitely applicable."

Jeremy continued and recounted Professor Teresa saying that about half of U.S. companies offer a 401(k) savings plan, which is similar to RRSPs in Canada, but employees are confused and do not know their price, their quality, or their danger.

Wanting to clarify what a 401(k) plan is in the United States, Jeremy referred to Wikipedia. He read:

> *A 401(k) plan, is the tax-qualified, defined-contribution pension account defined in subsection 401(k) of the Internal Revenue Code. Under the plan, retirement savings contributions are provided (and sometimes proportionately matched) by an employer, deducted from the employee's paycheque before taxation (therefore tax-deferred until withdrawn after retirement or as*

otherwise permitted by applicable law), and limited to a maximum pre-tax annual contribution of $18,000 (as of 2015).

Other employer-provided defined-contribution plans include 403(b) plans for non-profit institutions, and 457(b) plans for governmental employers. These plans are all established under section 401(a) of the Internal Revenue Code. 401(a) plans may provide a total annual addition of $53,000 (as of 2015) per plan participant, including both employee and employer contributions.

Jeremy reminded the group that company pension plans in the 1960's and 1970's were defined-benefit plans that used to provide secure income until death. In the 1980's, people started living longer, there were new accounting rules and global competition arrived. Market volatility increased the cost of maintaining a pension plan, as companies had to manage investment risk and manage longevity risk. They spent more money to fund plans if the market declined and they could actually lose money, then needed to fund more.

In the late 1970's and early 1980's, 401(k) plans were introduced, initially for high income earners, then for everyone. For employees, it opened up the opportunity to save for retirement in companies without a pension plan and allowed employees to have a portable vested amount of money to take with them when they changed jobs more frequently.

Companies now shared the responsibility for retirement saving with their employees instead of being solely responsible for employee pensions. Some employers contributed to 401(k) plans, but all of the risks fell on the employee. Thus, the defined-contribution plan replaced the defined-benefit plan for most companies.

Big brokerages and banks saw an opportunity to expand their businesses. In the early 1980's, the mutual fund industry realized there was a huge opportunity to sell mutual funds directly to individuals, and also make mutual funds the foundation of 401(k) plans.

With the stock market boom of the 1980's and 1990's, nobody noticed the high management fees being charged by the mutual fund companies.

The U.S. stock market topped in late 1999, then collapsed in the spring of 2000 to 1996 values. Some individuals had invested nineteen per cent of their money in their own company stock, and many of those companies folded or lost dramatically in the stock market crash.

"I was there," Jeremy explained, "when the 2008 housing and mortgage market crashed in the U.S. My wife and I, along with many other people, were forced to take money out of our savings and 401(k) plan."

Judit spoke up at this time. She said she was intrigued by Robert, the economist who spoke about mutual funds and securities on the documentary. She also provided a Wikipedia definition for mutual funds and securities:

> *A mutual fund is a professionally managed investment fund that pools money from many investors to purchase securities. While there is no legal definition of the term 'mutual fund', it is most commonly applied only to those collective investment vehicles that are regulated and sold to the general public.*
>
> *Mutual funds are generally classified by their principal investments. The four main categories of funds are money market funds, bond or fixed income funds, stock or equity funds, and hybrid funds. Funds may also be categorized as index funds (passively managed) or actively managed funds (traded).*
>
> *Investors in a mutual fund pay the fund's expenses, which*

reduce the fund's returns and performance. There is controversy about the level of these expenses.

A security is a tradable financial asset broadly categorized into:
debt securities, (e.g., banknotes, bonds and debentures)
equity securities, (e.g., common stocks)
derivatives, (e.g., forwards, futures, options and swaps).

Judit continued Robert's story. "He started saving in his company's 401(k) and noticed that there were no returns. He researched the companies invested in his mutual fund, then noticed all the fees. The average fee in the U.S. is 1.3 per cent; some charge two per cent up to five per cent. Canadian fees average over two per cent. Over twenty years, that really adds up.

"One of Robert's most disturbing findings was that mutual fund companies provide legal kickbacks to brokers for distributing and selling their funds. These kickbacks are paid by the investors—you and I—not the mutual fund company.

"In the spring of 2012, Robert's report, 'The Retirement Savings Drain: The Hidden & Excessive Costs of 401(k)'s', came out and received wide media attention including television and the financial press. He succeeded in raising public awareness of the high cost of mutual fund fees and the alarming effect these fees have on dramatically reducing our retirement savings."

Jeff was alarmed and upset by the story told by Jack Bogle, the founder of 'The Vanguard Group'. Jack used specific numbers to demonstrate the devastating effect of mutual fund fees on our savings:

"Assume you are invested in a fund earning seven per cent and are charged a two per cent annual fee. Over fifty years, the difference between your net (the five per cent), and what you would have made without fees (the seven per cent), is staggering! You have lost almost two-thirds (sixty-three per cent) of what you would have had. The magic of compound returns is overwhelmed by the tyranny of compounding costs. It's a mathematical fact. Ideally, you want to put up one hundred per cent of the capital, take one hundred per cent of the risk, and get thirty per cent of the return."

"For several years," Jeff explained, "Jack Bogle has been preaching the benefit of index funds that are passively managed. Since there is no trading or active management with index funds, these fees are not present, so the fee is only one per cent per year. This allows you to own all of the companies in the American (or Canadian) stock market directly. Jack says, *'You are then a creature of the market and not of the casino'.*"

Jackie took over and relayed comments from several people. "An analyst recommended that, *'All else being equal, you should buy the cheaper funds. A deeply guarded secret in the mutual fund industry is that many of the mutual fund managers own index funds.'*

"Year after year, in bull (up) and bear (down) markets, studies have overwhelmingly shown that actively managed mutual funds have failed to outperform index funds. Why aren't more people invested in low cost mutual funds?"

As a teacher, Jackie was shocked to learn that most retirement planners, financial planners, or financial advisors are merely brokers, or sales people. Only fifteen per cent are registered investment advisors or fiduciaries, who are obligated by law to act in their client's best interests.

She pointed out that broker dealers are not under that obligation. They only have to conform to a suitability standard, which means they cannot put you into something which is totally unsuitable for you. Their recommendation does not have to be the best for you, just suitable.

"Most 'planners'," she said, "will actually try to sell you the products that are most profitable for their own means. So, how do we tell when a financial advisor is really just a sales person?

We can ask them, 'Are you acting in my best interest? Would you be willing to sign a pledge that says that you are going to act as my fiduciary at all times with all products? If you're not, I'm going to leave'."

Jonathan added that he had experienced RRSP withdrawals and back end fees for those withdrawals, in addition to tax being withheld. He empathized with Mark, the unemployed sales manager on the documentary, especially when Mark was laid off, and he and his wife needed to withdraw some of their savings. Jonathan recounted his own parallels to Mark's story, and revealed how upset he was to discover there would be a fee of six hundred dollars from the mutual fund company to withdraw seven thousand dollars, in addition to the ten per cent tax that would be withheld.

Jeremy admitted he was encouraged, then disappointed when he heard that the U.S. Department of Labour tried to hold the industry accountable by proposing a new fiduciary rule in the fall of 2010. The rule would require all financial advisors to put their customers' interests ahead of their own whenever dealing with retirement accounts. The Labour Department eventually withdrew their proposal after tremendous lobbying by the financial services industry.

Jonquil thanked everyone for taking notes and sharing the information provided in 'The Retirement Gamble' documentary. She then gave Jeremy reason to be optimistic again, when she related what she found in the spring 2015 press. She explained that the top securities regulator in the U.S. announced plans to establish a higher standard, industry-wide. If these regulations were passed, they would certainly have an impact on Canadian regulators.

"In her first public remarks on the issue," Jonquil continued, "White, the chairwoman of the Securities and Exchange Commission (SEC) said that the SEC, should, 'implement a uniform fiduciary duty for broker-dealers and investment advisors, where the standard is to act in the best interest of the investor'.

"White's remarks came less than a month after U.S. President Barack Obama endorsed a similar proposal from the Labour Department to place all advisors and brokers on the more stringent fiduciary standard. According to a White House estimate, the conflicts of interest that arise in the absence of a uniform standard cost investors at least seventeen billion dollars each year.

"This will escalate a long-running battle between Wall Street and the administration over how to regulate the market for retirement advice. Critics of an expanded fiduciary duty say it would only serve to raise costs for brokers, forcing them to either raise prices for middle-class workers, or drop them altogether."

Jonquil noted that while the battle continues, investors are losing billions of dollars each year from misguided advice.

THE FINANCIAL SERVICES INDUSTRY BUSINESS MODEL

Continuing on from the learning in the documentary, Jonquil asked the group, "What is the financial services industry in business for?"

Jay jumped in and said, "To make money for their shareholders and stakeholders."

"Right on," said Jonquil. "Like any business, the goal of people in the financial services industry is to maximize profits. There is nothing wrong with this, provided you understand that they're playing a completely different game, with different rules than most people realize. They developed the entire industry in a way that increases their profits as their primary objective. Taking care of the individual investors is a secondary consideration."

Jonquil provided some facts for Canada. The financial services sector is a massive industry, creating roughly six per cent of Canada's entire GDP (Gross Domestic Product). Employing over

750,000 Canadians, the industry is a significant part of the economy, and very sophisticated. The sheer size gives it major influence when lobbying the government for laws and policies that benefit the companies involved in financial services.

She got into specifics regarding the financial services business model. "When you deposit money into your bank account, the bank turns around and lends out that money to someone else. It may be a mortgage, credit card limit, personal loan, or some other form of debt. They likely pay you nothing on your money unless you maintain a significant minimum balance, yet they are charging you anywhere from three per cent on mortgages, to as much as twenty-nine per cent on credit cards, when they lend out your money to another customer! That is basically what banks do. It's a great business model—borrowing something from one person at a very low rate, then turning around and lending that same asset out at a much higher rate . . . and making billions!

"Does it make sense that most people pay a monthly service fee to a bank for the privilege of holding onto their own money?" Jonquil asked, rhetorically. Then she used a startling comparison. "Imagine if you rented a spot at a parking lot, and each day when you parked there, the owner of the lot took your car and rented it to someone else. That's what the banking industry does with your money. No one complains because that's 'just the way it is'!"

LENDING MONEY THEY DO NOT HAVE

Jonquil asked the group to stand up and take a stretch before she dug deeper into, "things we weren't taught in school".

"What you probably don't know," Jonquil said after the break, "is that Canadian banks are legally allowed to lend money they don't actually have. Canada has the dubious distinction of being one of the few countries in the world that essentially allows its banks to lend out as much money as they want, without requiring them to have some amount of money backing their lending activity. The banks only need to keep a fraction of the deposits on hand as a reserve in order to meet the demands of any customer that might want some cash from their account.

"Canada used to employ a fractional reserve concept, where it would require a bank to have some amount of cash on deposit in order to back any loans or debts it was creating. In December 1991, the financial industry's lobbying power showed its strength and Bill C–19 was passed, which effectively eliminated the need for any reserves at all. This allowed the banks to charge fees and interest on money that doesn't even exist."

Jonquil paused. Some in the group had their mouths open in disbelief.

FINANCIAL SERVICES INDUSTRY MYTH BUSTERS

"What is a myth? Jonquil asked the group. Jordan was quick to respond. He Googled 'myth', and read out loud:

> *A myth is an idea or story that is believed by many people, but is not true.*

"I can tell you a myth," mocked Jonathan. "The financial services industry always has your best interest at heart." Everyone chuckled.

"Are you ready for some myth busters?" Jonquil asked.

"Bring them on," said Jenny.

Jonquil wrote each myth buster, in turn, on the flip chart.

Myth Buster #1:

Complicated investment products are good for business.
"As we confirmed earlier," she began, "the main objective for the

financial services industry is to create profits for its own shareholders first. This is accomplished by introducing a never-ending supply of financial products that can be sold to clients. By making these products increasingly more complex and adding hidden fees, commissions and charges, financial companies protect their very profitable model that continues to work.

"The industry will say, 'We don't hide our fees and commissions! They are in the 97-page prospectus that every investor is offered the chance to read'. The problem is," underlined Jonquil, "most investors aren't able to interpret a prospectus, because it is written in such complicated legal language."

Myth Buster #2:

Independent advice is almost impossible.

"You probably realize," said Jonquil, "that all Canadian banks have their own mutual funds and various investments they put together and sell. But did you know that they have salespeople responsible for selling those products? And do you know they are usually compensated more for selling 'in-house' products (the ones their bank offers) than the investments put together and offered by others?

"From a business perspective, this makes a lot of sense and is no different than other industries." Jonquil gave an example, "If you go into an Apple Store, you won't see a Dell computer as one of your options. Over the years, financial companies have figured out that it is far more profitable to put together investments, than it is to distribute and sell them.

"The best way to get unbiased advice," she told her avid audience, "is to find a fee-only financial planner, or advisor. They are called fee-only, because they charge a fee for the advice they give you. They don't earn commissions or fees from any investments they suggest for you. Only six per cent of all financial planners and advisors are fee-only, according to the 2008 Financial Planners Standards Council report, 'Profile of the Profession'.

"If you are looking for a financial planner or advisor, select from individuals who hold the 'CFP' (Certified Financial Planner) designation. This won't ensure the quality of your advisor; however, those who carry a CFP designation have gone through more education than non-CFP's and adhere to an industry code of ethics and standards."

Myth Buster #3:

Conflicts of interest exist between clients and commissioned salespeople.

Before expanding on this revelation, Jonquil first clarified some terms that are often used interchangeably.

A financial planner can be an important key to financial success, but there could be a problem. Most financial planners do not actually do any financial planning! They are too busy selling investments to worry about time-consuming financial plans.

A financial advisor is someone who holds a securities license and focuses on providing guidance for selecting investments. Their role is not to provide overall financial planning, but to assist in making investment decisions.

A stockbroker, whose job is to sell you investments such as stocks, does not even pretend to offer you financial planning advice.

Jonquil explained that the manner in which the financial industry is set up makes it difficult for planners, advisors and stockbrokers to serve their clients and themselves at the same time. Their goal is to create income for themselves by selling financial products and services to their clients. Most of them are compensated by commissions paid for by products they sell to you. Basically, if they do not sell investment products and services to you on a regular basis, they do not eat. While most salespeople hope to be able to generate positive returns for their clients, that is not the underlying motivation for many of them.

Myth Buster #4:

Advisors are often given sales quotas and told what to sell.
"Even more concerning," said Jonquil, "is that financial companies routinely manufacture an investment product, then direct their sales force, the advisors, planners or brokers, to go out and sell that product without knowing much about it."

Myth Buster #5:

Advisors do not even realize their damage to clients.
"The sad thing," said Jonquil, "is that most people assume that financial planners are experts, when in fact they have been taught mostly how to sell their products, not to analyze or understand them. A significant number of advisors and planners are not able to accurately calculate the real cost of hidden fees and expenses that are charged when you invest in certain kinds of investment products. Many are often unaware of the damage they are causing to their clients when they sell them investment products."

Myth Buster #6:

You may be more financially successful than your financial planner.
"This may be a shock to everyone," Jonquil stated, "but the average financial advisor, or financial planner in Canada makes approximately $49,000 per year. A 2009 Government of Alberta study revealed that the average financial planner's salary was $49,266.
"According to Pay Scale Inc., based on a survey of 586 respondents, the average annual salary of a personal financial advisor is $48,776. Those with the designation of CFP (Certified Financial Planner) earned an average of $51,190 per year.

"The financial industry has convinced the average Canadian that they need to take advice from anyone who calls themselves a 'planner' or 'advisor'. A proven principle in creating wealth is that you want to be learning from those that are achieving higher levels of success than you are. Listen to the people who are doing and receiving what it is that you want to do and receive," advised Jonquil.

She could tell that the group had learned a lot of information that they did not teach in the school system. It was time to ring the bell and end this week's class.

Next week they would go deeper into one of the financial service industry's most profitable products, mutual funds. "Your homework," said Jonquil, "is to research mutual funds, talk about your own experiences, and tell me how fees conflict with your quest to optimize savings growth for retirement."

Chapter 4:

MUTUAL FUND MYTHS AND SECRETS

"How many of you have invested in mutual funds?" asked Jonquil. Again, to her surprise, everyone but Jackie had invested in mutual funds, and most were still invested.

Jackie had her teacher's pension. She did not understand stocks or mutual funds, so stayed with low risk (she thought) GICs (Guaranteed Investment Certificates). She was correct that her initial investment was protected, so her principal was safe. However, she did not realize that the extremely low interest rate on her GIC's was making less than inflation, so she was actually losing money!

Jenny and Jeremy had redeemed their mutual funds to survive some hard knocks. Jeremy still had some money vested with his American employer in a 410(k) plan that was locked in until retirement.

Jenny was starting over after her divorce. She was disappointed with the lack of growth from her mutual funds that she had to redeem. Jenny was also frustrated by the high redemption fees that she had to pay in addition to the withholding tax. Now she was looking for a different investment vehicle to fund her retirement and was enjoying the energy and learning from the group.

Jonquil gave a brief overview of mutual funds—a popular investment vehicle that was created by, and is aggressively sold by, the financial industry. Her next statements got everyone's attention.

"Mutual funds rob more people of wealth and freedom than anything else! Canadians are investing in mutual funds without truly understanding what is going on behind the scenes."

Jonquil quoted Derek Bok who said, *'If you think education is expensive, try ignorance.'*

She then put the mutual fund industry in perspective. Over the past twenty years, individuals have handed over more than ten trillion dollars to the financial services industry. With the strong bull markets of the 1980's and 1990's, the mutual fund industry ramped up its advertising and promotions. People did not care about the fees they were paying. They did not have to pay attention. They got their quarterly statements and watched their savings grow.

Jeff agreed. He had enjoyed his mutual fund growth in the 1980's and 1990's, but that was over now. He was disappointed and frustrated by the current returns from his stock and bond mutual funds. He felt he had no control with wildly fluctuating markets and no alternative with the low interest rates. At the same time, he was held back from making any changes because of a lack of knowledge, uncertainty, and fear of getting outside of his comfort zone.

Jonathan had also invested in equity (stock) mutual funds in the 1980's and 1990's, and most of his funds did very well. Unfortunately, those days disappeared in the spring of 2000, when the stock market collapsed by fifty per cent. He hung in there while the market partially recovered, but did not like the wild swings that were occurring more and more frequently. He was looking for another investment vehicle and found an international investment that looked very profitable. Jonathan did his due diligence and contacted several other investors that had been in this investment for a few years. He listened to their stories of double digit interest rates each month and decided to invest.

Jonathan used most of his money outside his RRSPs and also money from a remortgaged second property to invest in this attractive investment. Each month he checked his investment online and was excited to see that it was growing rapidly. He was envisioning early retirement and enjoying more time freedom.

Then a year later, instead of reaping double-digit rewards, he was informed by the CSC (Canadian Securities Commission) that they were investigating the fund and the principal owner had gone missing. A few months after that, the police called to ask for an interview for testimony against the fund owners. They were gathering evidence from the many investors that were probably not getting their money back. Jonathan knew then that the odds of getting back his principal, let alone the interest, were slim to nil.

Jonathan had learned a big lesson. Some advisors are not honest from the start. Some advisors start out with honorable intentions, but then take an intentional wrong turn, leading their investors down a dead-end road and over a cliff. Jonathan got some consolation when he wrote off the principal; then, a few years later, used that capital loss from the bad investment to reduce the taxable capital gain on a property that he sold.

Jordan was complaining that his mutual funds were not growing. His financial advisor kept telling him that the funds were about even, since they went up fifty per cent and down fifty per cent over the last four years. On the surface that sounded reasonable, up and down by fifty per cent would balance each movement. However, he decided to look under the surface:

> With his thriving dental practice, Jordan was doing well and his initial investment was $100,000. The first year his mutual fund lost fifty per cent, so his fund was worth $50,000. The next year it gained fifty per cent to $75,000,

then lost fifty per cent again to $37,500, then gained fifty per cent to $56,250. In actuality, Jordan lost 43.75 per cent of his initial investment over four years!

Jordan did more calculations to see what would happen if his fund had gained fifty per cent in the first year instead of losing fifty per cent. Year one—up fifty per cent to $150,000; year two—down fifty per cent to $75,000; year three—up fifty per cent to $112,500; year four—down fifty per cent to . . . surprise . . . $56,250, the same value he ended up with in the first scenario. Either way, it was a loss of 43.75 per cent, and far from being 'even' as his financial advisor tried to tell him.

MANAGEMENT EXPENSE RATIO

While doing her research, Jonquil spoke with a lot of people. She was continually surprised by the number of people (at least three out of four), that did not know what a MER (Management Expense Ratio) was. This is the percentage of your investment that is deducted from your investment each year and paid to the mutual fund management team.

Jonquil gave an example. If a particular mutual fund carries a 2.5 per cent MER—that simply means that 2.5 per cent of the assets under management are paid to the manager each and every year. If your mutual fund was worth $100,000, at the end of the year, $2,500 would be deducted from your account for the 2.5 per cent management expense.

"Management expenses are not only for the management team of the mutual fund," she said. "Included in the MER are 'trailer fees', which is how the financial advisor, or planner that originally put you into the mutual fund, is compensated over time. In other words, your advisor generally continues to get paid as long as you stay in that specific mutual fund."

Jonquil quoted a May 2009 Fund Research Report from Morningstar regarding fees and commissions:

> *Assets tend to flow into average, or higher than average, fee funds because Canadian investors use financial advisors to help them make decisions. Advisors direct client assets to funds that pay better trailers. Since the trailer is included in the MER, the result is that assets flow into higher-fee funds.*

This appears to be a standard practice for investors because their financial advisors are 'helping' them make better decisions.

"Those recommendations," said Jonquil, "include funds with higher commissions! This seemingly 'fair' fee actually prevents financial freedom for many Canadians."

Jay was in shock, as he had trusted a financial advisor at his bank and invested in their bank mutual funds. He wanted a deeper understanding of what was going on with his mutual funds and asked Jonquil for an example with numbers.

Jonquil said, "You must have read my mind as that is exactly what I'm going to do." Using a flip chart to make her point, she wrote down the numbers as she walked the group through her example.

She continued, "You may be losing half of your returns from a 2.5 per cent fee! Let's look at an investor that has $100,000 to invest and decides to invest in a mutual fund with strong historical returns and a great management team. This miracle fund has generated gross returns averaging eight per cent a year, before taxes, for the past several years and charges a typical MER of 2.5 per cent."

As an aside, Jonquil said, "There are very few, if any, mutual funds that can claim an eight per cent long-term return. But I want you to see that, even when we use optimistic numbers, the results are still tragic." Jonquil went on to illustrate:

"Our investor takes the advice of the financial industry and invests $100,000 for a twenty year period, with the hope that they are going to build their nest egg into a nice little retirement fund for themselves and their family."

For her example, Jonquil used the very optimistic return of eight per cent gross per year. "Congratulations!" she said. "They should be rich now! An eight per cent return every year for twenty years is excellent, and should have grown the nest egg substantially.

"So... let's look at what would have happened if they had invested that $100,000 at an eight per cent return, but didn't pay any fees on it. Before fees, their $100,000 would have turned into $466,095.71, an increase of $366,095.01 over the original $100,000 after twenty years—impressive!

"Now... let's look at what happens when we include that small 2.5 per cent management fee in the mix. Believe it or not, after the 2.5 per cent fee is applied, their $100,000 turns into only $280,910.14; or an increase of only $180,910.14 over their original $100,000.

"Imagine," she exclaimed, "they lost over half (51%) of their potential return, simply because of a little 2.5 per cent fee they thought was reasonable! That little 2.5 per cent MER has reduced their overall return by more than $185,000!"

Jonquil explained that there are two places where the returns are diluted substantially.

"First of all," she explained carefully, "the 2.5 per cent fee actually ends up costing 25.2 per cent of your investment returns. Every year, the 2.5 per cent fee is charged against your entire investment account, even though you are only earning eight per cent."

She continued, "The reality is that you're not incurring a 2.5 per cent fee each year! You're actually paying out 2.5 per cent of the eight per cent total return that you make that year. This means the MER is actually costing you more than thirty-one per cent of your total investment returns. That 2.5 per cent fee on an eight per cent return is actually a fee of 31.25 per cent!" Jonquil circled that number on the flip chart.

"Secondly," she added, "every time the MER is removed from your account, you have lost the potential earnings you could have made from compounding, if that money had remained reinvested. The 2.5 per cent that you paid out in fees last year is not in your account to work for you this year. So, over time, this creates a significant loss of 25.4 per cent, because those expenses are being deducted and reducing the benefit of compound returns for you."

Jonquil emphasized that this example assumed a consistent eight per cent gross return by the mutual fund over twenty years. She said, "You'll spend a long time searching for this kind of return in the real world. Imagine what your returns would look like if you didn't achieve an eight per cent return, or worse, if your fund actually lost money!"

This new information was disturbing to everyone in the group. They were starting to understand why their funds were not performing up to their expectations. Jonathan had sensed that something was not right, but did not know the specifics. Jeff also knew that it was not like the old days when high returns hid high fees.

CANADIANS TOLERATE HIGH FEES

Jonquil was about to bring the discussion even closer to home. "Canada," she said, "is a nation quite tolerant of commitment and high fees. We readily sign long-term contracts regarding cell phones, cable television and mutual fund purchases. We pay higher fees than our U.S. neighbours. Why is this and, more importantly, will this ever change?" She looked around at the group of faces staring expectantly back at her.

"In relation to mutual funds, the first question is complex," she continued. "Canadians have traditionally not been well-versed regarding financial matters. Other than a few calculations in our high school math class, we are not routinely, or effectively, educated on the subject of money. We either become self-educated in adulthood, or place our trust in financial advisors."

Jonquil shared one glaring example of the public's lack of understanding in the mutual fund industry. "The deferred sales charge (DSC), is a back-end fee that is charged to a mutual fund investor if they redeem their investment prior to a set amount of time. It is a charge designed to discourage the early redemption, or sale, of your investment. A typical DSC starts at six per cent of your initial investment in year one and declines to zero per cent by year seven, effectively punishing an investor for selling their funds early.

"Mutual fund companies compensate their sales force (financial advisors) by paying them a commission for placing your money in their fund. The commissions can be as high as five per cent of your investment up front, plus half a per cent of the investment on an annual basis. Fund companies recoup this commission by charging an annual management fee on the investment, but it takes a few years to fully recoup it, and make a profit for themselves. The DSC was created to help soften the blow to the advisor if an investor leaves the fund early.

"If you purchased a mutual fund through an advisor at any time over the last decade without paying an out-of-pocket fee yourself," Jonquil said, "there is a high probability that you are in a fund with a DSC."

Jenny and Jeremy both nodded. They had found out about this charge the hard way, when they had to cash in their funds.

DEFERRED SALES CHARGE CONCERNS

Jonquil reviewed several problems that the DSC poses to mutual fund investors:

1. The DSC significantly increases the overall investment management fees. Paying a five per cent upfront fee to a salesperson, plus half a per cent per year, leaves mutual fund managers with a large expense to recover prior to making a profit for themselves. This invariably translates into higher fees paid by you, the investor.

2. DSCs give an incentive for an advisor to work hard to get their new clients into the investment, but then leaves little incentive to do any work after that. Once you have committed to the investment, your advisor has received the lion's share of their compensation and arguably has little direct motivation to continue fostering his or her relationship with you.

3. Perhaps, most important, is that the DSC locks you into a position for a very long time. If the investments do not perform as you expect, or you run into a need for cash, redeeming out of your funds will be a costly move.

There has been plenty of talk at the regulatory level about DSCs and fund commissions in general. Jonquil found out that Britain and Australia have indirectly banned the practice, but no such action has emerged in Canada or the U.S.

REDUCED FEE OPTIONS

Fortunately, the public is becoming more aware, and individuals are increasingly scrutinizing the fee options associated with mutual funds. According to InvestorEconomics.com, no-load funds and back-end funds that do not require a front-end or back-end fee now account for over seventy-one per cent of gross mutual fund sales in Canada.

Jonquil had found a few options for investors that want to invest in mutual funds, but are not interested in getting locked into a DSC; especially one that runs on a sliding scale, involving fees if they withdraw their money within a certain period of time. These options included:

1. **Discount brokers**
   Invest online on your own through a discount broker. The upside is that you will not be locked into a DSC; but the downside is that you will not get any advice, or necessarily cut down your fund's overall management expense ratio (MER).

2. **Front-end loads**
   Request that your advisor places you into front-end loads. The upside is that you will avoid the DSC and you will get professional advice. The downside is that you will have to pay out-of-pocket for an upfront commission to your advisor. Most advisors charge two per cent upfront commission. However, depending on how much money you are investing, you may be able to negotiate this commission downward.

3. **No-load funds**
   These funds are essentially DSCs, but with less punishing term—usually a two to three-year lock-in. They pay the advisor a smaller commission, but it is still higher than what they would get with a front-end load fund. This may be a good option for investors with smaller amounts of money who still want a financial advisor, but are not interested in locking into traditional DSC's.

4. **F-class funds**
   Brokers typically reserve this service for clients with higher minimum asset levels. This allows the client and advisor to negotiate a set annual fee, and any commissions or annual trailer fees are not paid to the advisor. This is a great option for investors who want to use an advisor and want controlled access to their investments. Depending on your level of assets under management, fees typically range from half a per cent to two per cent per year. Fees charged in a non-registered

account are normally tax deductible, adding to the benefits of this option.

Judit was very discouraged. She and her husband had worked hard. She had started a savings account as a teenager and graduated to mutual funds in her early twenties. Now she was starting to understand what was happening and why her funds were not growing as expected. The mutual fund myths were unraveling.

MUTUAL FUND MYTHS

"Mutual funds advertise and promote several benefits," Jonquil said, "So let's take a closer look at these 'benefits'. Are they really benefits, or myths?"

The group knew all about myths from their discussions the previous week.

Myth #1: Convenience

Jonquil agreed that it is convenient to invest in mutual funds, but she compared such convenience to going for fast food three times a day, rather than trying to eat a healthy, balanced meal. The reality is that anytime you choose an investment option for convenience, you are probably not making the best financial decision you can.

Myth #2: Saves Time

With her research experience, Jonquil said she certainly understands that it takes time for an investor to do their own research and comprehend what they are investing in. The financial industry built it that way. It does take more time to be an active, intelligent investor, but the choice you are making is not one of time management. You are trading away your financial potential, when you take the lazy approach and invest in something simply because you do not want to take the time to really understand what you are doing.

Myth #3: Professional Money Management

"On the surface," Jonquil responded, "this seems like a logical argument. Why try to manage your own money when you can let a professional do it for you? If it was that simple, active money management by professionals would make sense."

There are a number of reasons why this logic does not hold true. If mutual fund managers are so much smarter than the average person, why is it that approximately eighty per cent of all mutual funds underperform the market after fees?

Another question to ask is, "If professional money managers are so great at investing, why aren't they all super rich and retired?" Actively managed funds do not outperform a static basket of stocks. There is no scientific evidence that mutual funds will outperform the market. As Jack Bogle said in 'The Retirement Gamble' documentary, *'Buy the least cost alternative, Index Funds —ones that buy and hold a broad spectrum of stocks that match a stock market index and you only pay one per cent'.*

Myth #4: Diversification

"This is the same as 'don't put all your eggs in one basket'," said Jonquil.

That seems like good advice; however, in the investment world it is dangerous advice and usually leads to mediocre returns.

Warren Buffet, the billionaire investor, says that wide diversification is only required when investors do not understand what they are doing. In the investment world, you need to understand what you are investing in and focus your efforts. Spreading your money around into fifteen different asset classes and not understanding any of them is a recipe for disaster. Unfortunately, that is what the financial industry wants you to do, because they make more money as a result.

Myth #5: Transferability

"At first glance," Jonquil said, "this suggests that, because you can move your money around into different funds a particular company has, you get flexibility. If you don't like the fund you're invested in, you can switch it over to one of the other funds that company owns. The challenge is, what if all of their funds are not good investments? When you restrict your choices to only those that are offered by one company, you significantly reduce your chances of success."

The group mood seemed to be changing from anger and frustration, to interest and pursuit of knowledge. Judit exclaimed, "Let's learn more about mutual funds. What else do we need to know?"

Jonquil responded by teasing them. "Let's look at some industry secrets," she told them.

"Secrets can be intriguing and important to know," acknowledged Jordan.

MUTUAL FUND SECRETS

1. Not in Business to Make You Money

Jonquil reminded them of the financial industry priorities they had discussed last week, and how the documentary had also underscored this issue. Most people think the primary goal of every fund manager is to help people make money. In reality, whether your funds make money, or whether they do not, makes no difference to them, since they get paid their fees regardless of whether you gain or lose. This is an example of how the financial industry places itself in direct conflict with the interests of the individual investor.

The primary objective of every mutual fund manager is to accumulate as many assets under management as possible. Since the manager takes a percentage of all the assets they manage, their primary objective is to attract as much investment capital into the fund as possible. Once there, and as long as they keep those investments from leaving, they continue to make their management fees on the entire pool of funds.

"Do you see the problem?" Jonquil asked. "They take very little risk and get a predictable return, while you invest your money and take all the risk of loss!"

"What a rip!" Jay exclaimed.

2. Canadians Pay Highest Fees

This next revelation was shocking to everyone, although Jeremy, a U.S. citizen, was chuckling. Jonquil had previously asked the question, "Why do Canadians put up with the highest expenses in the world?"

According to Morningstar's Fund Research Report from May 2009, based on the research of sixteen developed countries, Canada has the highest fees in the world for mutual funds. The report states:

> *The typical investor in a Canadian equity fund pays a MER of between two per cent and two and a half per cent. Canadian investors do not pay much attention to fees. Canadian investors are comfortable with the fees because they do not know how low these fees should actually be.*

Jonquil continued, "Canadian cell phone expenses are also among the highest in the developed world. It would seem that we are just too polite, or timid, to demand better value for the services and products we purchase. We are also willing to trust our big financial institutions much more than any other country."

Jonathan jumped in emphatically, "One contributing factor is that our education system does a poor job teaching people the basics of money. The financial industry then picks up where the education system leaves off, and keeps investors like us in the dark about some of the most important and crucial elements of understanding an investment. This leads not only to record profits for the financial industry, but to devastating financial futures and retirements for Canadians! I say 'kudos' to Jonquil for pulling back the curtain and exposing these secrets!"

3. MERs Plus More Fees

Jonquil was enjoying revealing these secrets. She had worked diligently on her research and was proud to help her fellow investors become more enlightened and spread the word.

The MER covers management costs and marketing expenses of the fund. But, there are also industry 'trading costs'—additional expenses that cover things not included in the MER.

Brokerage Fees

Every time the fund manager executes a trade, or buys or sells stocks or investments inside the fund, a commission is paid. The average fund turns over about eighty per cent of their portfolio per year, so these costs can add up significantly and have a material impact on the net results of the fund.

Market Impact Costs

When a mutual fund has a huge holding of a particular asset, and tries to sell off that large holding quickly, market impact costs occur. Depending on the liquidity of the asset, the bid/ask price may be high, which increases the cost to make the trade. Jonquil translated, "This means the fund manager may have to pay more than the going price to acquire a large block of shares. If selling, they may have to accept a lower price, because there are fewer buyers willing to take on that amount of stock at the going rate."

Sales Charges

According to Investor Economics, about seventy-five per cent of funds in Canada have sales charges (loads), either front-end or deferred. Front-end charges are charged to the investor when the investment is first made. Deferred charges are incurred when the investment is sold. Most investors never hold a fund for seven years, so they end up paying some amount of deferred charge when they sell.

Jonquil continued, "What these added expenses end up costing investors is difficult to estimate, but a 2007 analysis by Virginia Tech, the University of Virginia, and Boston College revealed that the average additional cost to an investor, over and above the MER, is 1.44 per cent per year. That means if a mutual fund has a MER of 2.5 per cent, the real cost to the investor is close to four per cent once these additional, sometimes hidden, costs are factored in! Who knew!" she exclaimed.

4. Funds Do Not Follow Their Own Advice

"This secret is almost comical," Jonquil chuckled. "Mutual fund managers don't take the same advice that the financial industry gives to individual investors. The classic mantra is that you should buy an investment and hold onto it for the long-term—referred to as 'buy-and-hold' investing."

Jonathan was very familiar with this slogan. He had invested in a major Canadian mutual fund family that proclaimed as their tagline: 'Buy. Hold. Prosper'.

Another piece of advice the industry gives to clients is, 'don't try to time the market'. Jonquil explained, "This means buying stocks that you think are going to go up in the short term and selling stocks you think may decline for whatever reason."

When you look at the mutual fund industry, you rarely find anyone practicing this investment wisdom. With an approximate eighty per cent turnover of their portfolio per year (meaning they are selling eighty per cent of what they own), many of these trades are done with a short-term view, going against both the market timing advice and the buy and hold advice that most financial advisors dispense.

"Guess what this results in?" inquired Jonquil.

"Higher trading expenses for the fund, and reduced returns for me," said Judit.

"You're absolutely correct," responded Jonquil, "since commissions are paid every time a transaction takes place inside the fund. And, because these trading expenses are not included in the fund's MER, they further reduce your net returns!"

5. More Mutual Funds than Stocks

"Amazingly, there are approximately three times as many Canadian mutual funds as there are individual stocks that trade in Canada" said Jonquil. "Over nine thousand mutual funds, including ETF's (Exchange Traded Funds), hedge funds and traditional mutual funds dwarf the three thousand individual stocks that trade on the Toronto and Montreal exchanges."

Jonquil explained, "The problem with this is that many of the mutual funds are very similar and own similar investments, since there are only so many investments that a multi-billion-dollar investment fund can make. Choices are generally restricted to the biggest Canadian stocks. The plethora of mutual fund choices ends up creating duplication and confusion for an investor."

6. Mutual Funds Must Always Be Fully Invested

"This was a surprise to me," said Jonquil. "Many mutual funds are mandated to remain 'fully invested' at all times. What this really means is that they are not allowed to sit on a large percentage of cash in their portfolio, because their fund objective does not list cash as a major component.

"On the surface this makes logical sense, since it allows an investor to see what that fund intends to invest in, and whether the manager intends to hold any cash inside the fund. However, this ends up working against a mutual fund investor, because it restricts the manager's ability to respond to the marketplace."

Jonquil used 2008 as an example. A fund manager would have done very well by putting their fund into an all-cash position early in the decline. Unfortunately, they were unable to do this, because their fund guidelines required them to leave the vast majority of the fund invested in the market.

They are forced to go out and find 'the best of the worst', because their money has to remain invested. They can only try to pick investments that are 'less bad" than the alternatives. This partly explains why Canadian mutual funds lost an average of more than twenty per cent in 2008, according to the Investment Funds Institute of Canada.

7. Historical Performance Was Worse Than Presented

"Have you ever seen mutual funds ads in magazines and newspapers trumpeting their amazing one-year or three-year returns?" asked Jonquil. Most of the group raised their hand. "Well, the reality is that those numbers rarely reflect the big picture, so stay tuned," she said.

Mutual fund managers recognize that most of their investors are not sophisticated and are attracted primarily by impressive returns. As a result, these fund managers devise creative ways to improve their 'historical returns' to attract more investors.

Mutual fund companies have a range of different investment funds and, over time, some of those funds underperform. When it becomes obvious that a fund is a loser, the manager will close that fund down and stop reporting those historical returns. The industry refers to this as 'survivorship bias', which simply means that the returns you see quoted do not really reflect all of the company's investment funds—only the funds they have not closed because they underperformed!

Jonquil explained, "When a fund is closed down, returns from that fund no longer need to be disclosed to investors, so the historical returns quoted by a company are only the returns of the funds doing well. This skews the overall track record of the company to be higher than it really was. If not shut down, these underperformers get merged into more successful funds to hide their poor performance."

Chasing high historical returns in the mutual fund industry is always a bad idea, because studies have shown that when a fund is a leader in its class one year, it almost always falls out of the lead position the next year.

"So don't invest in a fund because it produced high returns the previous year!" warned Jonquil. "Amazingly, this is still how most mutual fund investors, and many financial advisors, decide which funds to invest in and recommend."

"Are there any more secrets?" Judit asked. "I think I've seen enough of mutual funds for a while!" she said with a yawn.

"No more secrets tonight," replied Jonquil. "I hear a lot of frustration and lack of understanding from the group, so I think it's time to step back and think about an often overlooked piece of the puzzle.

Next week, we'll talk about attitude, hoping and praying, due diligence and responsibility. Please be prepared to talk about your experiences trying to answer question two: How do you invest that money? Have a safe trip home, everyone!"

Chapter 5:

ATTITUDE AND RESPONSIBILITY

"Last week I heard a lot of frustration when you were talking about your experiences trying to answer question two: How do you invest that money?" Jonquil said. "Let's get the emotion of that frustration and lack of knowledge out in the open."

Judit was still very discouraged and angry. She started a savings account as a teenager and transitioned to mutual funds in her early twenties. She and her husband worked hard to save. She was starting to understand why her mutual funds were not growing as expected. "Now what?" she exclaimed. "I put all my eggs in the mutual fund basket and it looks like those eggs may never hatch!"

Jeremy had some money vested in his 410(k) plan, but that was locked in until retirement. He had to redeem his other savings. Much of it went to pay for his wife's medical expenses when they lived in the U.S. "What do I do now?" he moaned. "I don't know where to start."

Jenny was starting over after her divorce and was upset by her hard knocks. Her funds had not grown much; then she had to redeem them. The icing on the cake was when she had to pay the high redemption fees just to get her own money back! "I'm a nurse and I help other people every day," she blurted out. "When it comes to finances, I'm on my own now. That's why I joined this group for advice and support."

Jeff really enjoyed his mutual fund growth in the 1980's and 1990's, but that was long gone. "I have no control over the unpredictable stock markets these days, and there really is no alternative with the low interest rates," he complained. "I don't know of any other options and, quite frankly, I'm afraid of getting outside of my comfort zone."

Jackie was also afraid of doing anything different. She had her teacher's pension and did not understand stocks or mutual funds. "When I found out from the group that I was actually losing money on my GICs, I freaked," she exclaimed. "What do I do now? Can I count on my teacher's pension alone, since I was off for several years raising my three kids?"

Jonathan, like Jeff, had enjoyed the growth of his stocks and mutual funds in the 1980's and 1990's, but unlike Jeff, he started investing in real estate. The stock market collapse of 2000 dropped his portfolio by fifty per cent as his growth funds were hit hard. "Then I was on an emotional roller coaster with that international investment that looked great at first, then fell off the cliff," he lamented. "I kept beating myself up and it took a long time to get over it." Since then, he has been exploring other investment avenues, including real estate.

Jordan's experience with his mutual funds was like playing with a yoyo, fifty per cent up and fifty per cent down. The lack of empathy, or recommendations, from his financial advisor was reaching a breaking point. "I make good money," he said. "So why do I throw it away on mutual funds? There must be a better investment vehicle, and I'm here to find it!"

Jay was still in shock that he had trusted a financial advisor from his bank and invested in their proprietary bank mutual funds. "I'm the new kid here and I'm listening hard. I appreciate you older folks showing me what not to do," he said half-jokingly.

The others knew that he could also help them with his online skills and sharp mind.

Jonquil waited until everyone had told their stories and had a chance to let off steam. "Thanks everyone, great stories!" she said. "I appreciate your candidness and feel your frustration. I've been there too!"

Jonquil then told the group how she wrote stories for the local paper in high school and put her savings into a bank account. She took journalism at university, worked part-time writing blogs and online banner copy for businesses, and started investing in mutual funds. After graduation she continued writing blogs and online banner copy, got a full-time job at a local newspaper, and started investing in equity stocks.

She admitted she became frustrated watching her stocks and mutual funds go up and down, and started investigating. "I was determined to take matters into my own hands and learn as much as I could behind the scenes," she said. A friend of hers was making money investing in real estate, so Jonquil started broadening her research.

"My increasing interest and knowledge landed me a job as a writer with Wealth magazine. When I saw that documentary, 'The Retirement Gamble', it really stirred me up," she said. "I decided right then and there that I was going to do a story on retirement and assemble a group of diverse people to help me with it. So here we are!"

NOBODY TAKES CARE OF YOUR MONEY BETTER THAN YOU

Jonquil told the group that an important part of the story is attitude. She practiced tough love on herself and shared her thoughts with the group. "Until you are willing to identify and take responsibility for negative investment outcomes, you will be powerless to stop them, because you are in the role of victim," she said.

"Blindly throwing money at an investment without understanding it is no different than betting in Las Vegas," she continued.

"Anytime you put money toward something that you don't understand, you're gambling, not investing."

Most investors are putting their money into investments they have no knowledge or understanding of, so it is not surprising that most investors do not have much success.

Jonquil found a report in the Toronto Star by financial reporter, Ellen Roseman, about a survey of Canadian investors in mutual funds. Of those surveyed, sixty percent did not know what an MER (Management Expense Ratio) was, and forty per cent could not name the fund they were invested in. "Imagine that! Forty per cent of investors didn't even know what it was that their money was invested in!" Jonquil exclaimed. "That's like having money invested in real estate, but not knowing in what city or province it is in."

Sadly, most people never take the time to learn anything about how investing, finance, or money works. They simply listen to the experts, hand their money over to others who claim to be professionals, and hope for the best. For many people, investing and money management are some kind of weird magic, and they choose to not understand it. It is too painful to try and learn it, so they avoid the topic—and their financial statements reflect this.

HOPE AND PRAY

Jonquil traced the progression of this lack of financial knowledge throughout most people's lives. You grow up and get through high school and, possibly college or university, or go directly into the workforce. You become acutely aware of all the financial things you know nothing about. You begin to hear about the stock market, RRSPs, mutual funds, real estate, taxes, corporations, stockbrokers, cash flow, contribution matching, market timing, diversification, dollar-cost averaging, and others.

Since you have never formally been taught any of these things, they cause you anxiety and concern, because you have no idea what they are or what you should be doing about them. As you accumulate some money, you have a sense that you should be doing something with that money, but you really do not know what to do. You feel overwhelmed trying to figure out what to do. Fear and worry set in.

"Your parents aren't able to offer any intelligent advice and your friends don't seem to understand things any more than you do, so you do what most people do in this situation and turn to a financial advisor to ask for some help. And the story begins," continued Jonquil.

"You feel a sense of relief as you hand your responsibilities over to an expert who will take care of your money. When you meet with him or her, they sound very smart and gain your confidence that you selected the right person. Since you don't know what to ask, they don't discuss their compensation, or how they are going to profit from working with you. The nature of your relationship with them is rarely discussed in detail. All you know is they're going to manage your money and grow it so you can enjoy a wonderful retirement.

"Then you basically ignore your financial situation, trusting it to someone else. You don't educate yourself, or learn about new products and services coming into the marketplace. You don't pay attention to the fundamentals of the markets. You can't, because you wouldn't know where to start.

"You continue with your career or your business, your family and all the other priorities you have. You have enough going on in your life and the last thing you need to do is try to become a financial expert. You've never been good with numbers and it's not your skill set. You do what you need to do, your advisor manages your money, and everyone lives happily ever after."

"Right" said Jenny, sarcastically.

"Unfortunately," Jonquil nodded, "it rarely works out that way! At some point, most investors find out that while this fairytale is easy to believe, it usually doesn't come true. Eventually, some kind of financial problem arises. There is a meltdown in the stock market, interest rates increase without warning, or your portfolio takes a hit for some reason that you are not clear on.

"You look to your advisor for help and reassurance, and they tell you, 'Don't worry! Now is not the time to panic. You're in it for the long haul and this is a terrible time to pull out.' They tell you the market will come back and try to calm you down.

"You feel trapped, because you do not have any idea how to interpret what is going on and you are blindly relying on someone you hope knows what they are doing. You feel overwhelmed, because you don't know whether you should change your advisor, or stick with them for the long run. You blindly trust others with your money and do not become educated so you can make better decisions in the future.

"For many investors," Jonquil said, "this cycle repeats itself for their entire lifetime, over and over again. Some investors switch advisors during a downturn, while others stick with theirs, hoping that at some point things will turn around. This is the popular investing for retirement strategy of most Canadians—the 'hope and pray' strategy. They are simply hoping and praying that things are going to turn out okay," she said. "You're still here so you already know this is a fairytale."

Hoping and praying is what you have to do if you decide to hand over your money to someone and let them take care of it. You have to hope they know what they are doing, and pray they make decisions in your best interest so you do not lose it all.

ATTITUDE

Jonquil warned, "Being a victim can be so damaging to your net worth and your retirement. Choose not to be a victim anymore. Realize that your attitude is as important, if not more important, than learning about investment principles, facts and figures."

A few years ago, Jonquil learned to stop being a victim with her money and investing. "How did I do this?" she posed the question to the group. "By asking myself, 'what role did I play in this?' This question immediately takes me out of the victim mentality and places me squarely in reality. It forces me to think about what role I played in the outcome and helps me avoid the trap of blaming and justifying."

Jonquil continued, "By asking yourself this question, it forces you to be accountable for at least some part of the outcome. The more you ask this question and the more you honestly answer it, the more you begin to realize that you, not someone or something else, is primarily responsible for the outcome."

Jonquil stated that she believes that a direct indicator of how successful you will be in life and in retirement, not just financially, is based on your willingness to accept responsibility for yourself and be accountable for your results.

"To be successful, you must immediately begin assuming responsibility and be accountable for all the negative things that you have in your life," she said. "The more you can eliminate blame and justification from your vocabulary, the more successful you'll be."

Jonquil continued, "The moment that I became accountable, my life changed. You have that very same opportunity. You simply need to make the decision."

YOUR 'WHY'

"Another key step to success," said Jonquil, "is knowing your 'why'. Most people ask, 'what is that investment going to do for me?' This is a sign that they are looking outside of themselves and want their investment to 'save' them."

Jonathan pointed out something he had learned. "You don't ask a successful person how they became successful. You ask them 'why'; their answer to 'why' is where you find the gold. It will reveal their burning desire to overcome all odds and be successful at whatever they do or invest in."

"The first step to becoming a successful investor and preparing for your retirement is to clearly understand that the motivation for investing is not money," said Jonquil. "That might seem contradictory, but belies the truth that, if you focus on chasing money, you will be like a dog chasing a squirrel and never quite catching it."

When you focus on creating a clear vision of exactly what investing will provide you, then you will be driven to achieve your dream. You will avoid distractions and overcome hurdles along the way, to stay focussed.

Your vision, if it is compelling, will be the first thing you think of when you get up, and the last thing you think of before you go to sleep. It will keep you going even when you hit roadblocks, and drive you forward when others around you question what you are doing.

"It is everyone's intention to live a happy and satisfying life," said Jonquil. "You can build on that basic intention. Look clearly within yourself to see what you really want out of your life and what you want to give in return.

"Ask yourself more questions:
- What would leave me completely fulfilled and satisfied?
- What impact do I want to have on the people in my life?
- If I had $500 million, what would I do once I helped myself and those around me?"

Jonquil asked everyone to work on their 'why' over the next week, by pretending that it is five years from today. "Describe, in writing, as detailed as you can, what you achieved over those five years. Make it real. Visualize it in your mind. Create a collage on a piece of cardboard by pasting pictures from magazines or the internet. Have fun with it.

"Your collage will answer the questions: What has investing for my retirement five years ago given me now? Where do I live? Who do I spend my time with? What hobby or business do I spend time on? Do I travel; if so, where? How is my health? What is my fitness and nutrition program? How much have I saved for retirement? What music, books and art am I enjoying? Who am I helping? How am I making a difference?"

INSTINCT AND INVESTOR BIASES

Jonquil shared some of her research on human behavior. "As humans," she said, "we have instincts, habits and responses that evolved over thousands of years, with the sole purpose of helping us to survive in a dangerous world."

She uncovered a key finding for investors. "The way our brains are wired is in direct conflict with good investment habits. These problem instincts are investor biases. A 'bias' is simply a false judgment or assumption that is not based on fact, or truth. I've always been intrigued by what causes people, including myself, to do foolish things like holding onto a stock after it's dropped with little hope of ever coming back," said Jonquil. "Why do investors buy real estate at the very top of the market, thinking they're getting in at the bottom, when market indicators clearly say otherwise?

"Well, psychologists have proven that we only do something for one of two primary reasons:

1. to obtain pleasure or
2. to avoid pain.

"They've also proven that our instinct to avoid pain is much stronger than our desire for pleasure," said Jonquil. "Your brain will go out of its way to avoid pain regardless of whether there's an opportunity to obtain pleasure. This is hardwired into us as human beings."

Bias #1: The Need to be Right

"One of the most powerful human instincts instilled in us is that each of us has a deep desire to be right about the decisions we make. We get a sense of pleasure when we are correct. Conversely, when we are wrong, we experience a degree of psychological pain, so we try to avoid being wrong.

"Most investors are afraid of losing," Jonquil continued. "They take a profit whenever they can and that sure profit violates the investing rule of 'letting your profits run.' The reverse is also true, holding on to save face instead of selling when the stock is falling."

Jeff and Jonathan both experienced this with Nortel stock in 2000. Jonathan bought some Nortel shares at thirty-five dollars per share and more at sixty-five dollars. Jeff started buying at seventy-three dollars a share. Both investors held onto it while the stock price ran up to over one hundred and twenty dollars per share. They still held it while it dropped like a stone to twelve dollars; then both sold at a huge loss.

"Something told me to sell earlier," said Jonathan, "but that would mean accepting that I was wrong to hold on. In hindsight, this was one of my greatest learning experiences as an investor."

Jeff agreed. His pain lasted for several months, but he learned the lesson of accountability and realized how dangerous the need to be right can be as an investor. "It is often when we take a loss or make a mistake that we truly grow and evolve as human beings and investors," Jeff said. "Through these difficult experiences we learn how the investment world really works."

Bias #2: Overconfidence

"A dangerous bias is overconfidence that comes in many forms," said Jonquil.

An investor makes decisions out of courage, or a false belief that they know more about the situation or strategy than they really do.

Studies show that eighty per cent of all drivers rank themselves as 'better than average' when surveyed about their driving abilities. Of course, this is impossible. Many of those surveyed are incorrect and would actually fall in the 'worse than average' category. Most drivers do not accept this and assume they are better drivers than they really are, exhibiting overconfidence on the road.

Another cause of overconfidence is the illusion of control. Many investors incorrectly believe they have more control over a given situation than they actually do, leading them to make decisions based on bad assumptions.

Jonquil pointed to the lottery industry that demonstrates how profits are made by taking advantage of human biases such as the illusion of control. When you buy a ticket for Lotto 6/49, you have the choice of allowing the computer to select your numbers, or you can choose your own 'lucky numbers' for the draw.

"What do most people do?" she asked. "As the overconfidence bias predicts, most people prefer to choose their own numbers because they feel they're more in control of their odds of winning. Logically, we know that the odds are identical, but most people don't stop to think about this so the lottery industry makes billions of dollars as a result."

Another overconfidence challenge that many investors do not see coming is early success, or 'beginners luck'. This is often the worst thing that can happen to an investor. It causes new investors to quickly think they are more capable and talented at investing than they really are.

That was the case with Jeff when he kept buying more and more Nortel stock. It was his first entry into the stock market. Jeff's early success lead him to take bigger and bigger risks and put him in a position where he ended up taking a loss he could not afford.

In an ideal world, we would eliminate our emotions from any decisions involving money. Unfortunately, as we know, that is impossible. So, the only way to create success and prosperity is to:

1. understand what you are investing in, and
2. reduce, as best you can, the biases and instincts that always work against you.

Jonquil made this suggestion, "Instead of trying to eliminate emotions from your decision-making, focus on identifying when you're letting emotions and biases take over and learn to manage them. This could be one of the best lessons you learn, to take control of your finances and your retirement!"

RESPONSES TO NEGATIVE OUTCOMES

Jonquil relayed to the group that there are three possible responses to negative outcomes.

1. Blame

We place blame on someone or something other than ourselves for the negative outcome. This is the primary method in which most investors respond to losses.

2. Justify

We try to find good reasons for why it happened beyond our control. Investors attempt to justify the outcome and just shrug their shoulders.

3. Take Responsibility

We take responsibility for the outcome. Investors accept that the reason for the negative outcome was in whole or in part due to the actions or inactions they took personally.

In the first two responses, the power is in the hands of someone or something else. You cannot control the outcome. You are a victim and it is not your fault; therefore, it must be the fault of someone or something else. In the third response, you are forced to step up and recognize that you played a role in the negative outcome. Most investors do not like to do this. It is much easier to point the finger at someone else, or come up with a good reason or excuse why things did not turn out as planned.

"This week was an important step to expose emotions, observe attitudes, determine your why and take responsibility. When we're prepared to take responsibility for our knowledge and our actions," said Jonquil, "we can look at other investment options.

"Really work on your 'why' over the next week; make that collage and keep those all-important questions in mind while you are doing it. You might just discover some interesting things about yourself in the process. Since this is a very powerful and very personal project, we will not be discussing this as a group. Hopefully, it will motivate you to make changes, overcome obstacles, maintain focus and prepare yourself for retirement.

"Next week we'll talk about the pros and cons of real estate as an investment vehicle. Please be prepared to talk about any experiences you have had with real estate. That may include your own home, a vacation property, an investment property, or anything else related to real estate. Have a safe trip home!"

Chapter 6:

WHY REAL ESTATE?

"Did you know," asked Jonquil, "that most millionaires achieved their financial success with real estate?" She continued, "Over ninety per cent of the world's wealthiest people control real estate!"

That immediately got everyone's attention, even Jordan, who had arrived late because of traffic, and was just sitting down.

Jonquil followed with a quote from one of the best investors of our time, Warren Buffet, who said, *'the best time to invest in real estate was thirty years ago; the next best time is today!'*

"How many of you have invested in real estate?" Jonquil queried.

Everyone but Jay raised their hands.

"Okay, great!" she said. "Now, if you don't count your principal residence, by that I mean your home, how many of you have invested in real estate?"

Only two hands went up, Jonathan's and Jenny's.

"Perfect! Let's hear your story first, Jenny," Jonquil said.

Jenny was quick to start telling her story of their home and investment property that had to be sold when she went through her divorce. "My husband and I joined a real estate investment club that met every month and learned the basics. We enjoyed the networking and learning from other investors. The only downside was the almost two hour drive to get to the meetings," she said. "We were doing well and bought an investment property a few years ago to diversify our investments," she continued. "Our mutual funds were up and down and we were learning more and more about the opportunities with real estate."

Jenny got excited as she remembered their discovery at one of the first investment club meetings. "The light went on for both of us," she said, "when we realized that we could buy a second property, rent it out, and make money three different ways by:

1. paying down the mortgage to reduce the debt,
2. positive cash flow, and
3. appreciation."

This got the group's attention and curiosity. Jay asked Jenny to expand on these three ways of making money in real estate.

"Sure," she said. "I'll start with the second one, positive cash flow. I'm no expert, but I'll do my best. I definitely want to get back into real estate investing on my own as soon as I can."

Jonquil jumped up and said, "I'll help you, Jenny. I've been researching this investment vehicle and have an investment property myself." Jonquil started writing on the flip chart so everyone could see what Jenny was explaining.

POSITIVE CASH FLOW

"The most important thing to me," Jenny said, "is to ensure that you are bringing in more income than your expenses every month. That is called 'positive cash flow'."

Jonquil wrote an example on the flip chart of a landlord receiving $1,600 in rent each month and paying out $1,273 in expenses.

That would be a positive cash flow of $1,600 - $1,273 = $327 each month.

"Rent is easy to understand," Jordan said, "but what's included in the expenses?"

Jonquil cautioned, "Before we talk about expenses, always look for other possible avenues of additional income such as rental of a garage, parking space or storage area, laundry income and income from offering additional services such as internet. Sometimes, these items can be rented separately from the rental unit."

"For simplicity," Jenny said, "we'll use a single family home as one rental unit to review expenses." Jonquil listed the expenses on the flip chart.

There are two basic ways to calculate expenses:

1. If the tenant pays for utilities (included in their rent or added onto their rent), then utilities are not included in your expenses
2. If the tenant does not pay for utilities then they are included in your expenses

Utilities:
- Heat (gas, oil, electric, hot water)
- Electricity
- Sewer and Water

Expenses Before Debt Service:
- Property taxes
- Insurance
- Repairs and Maintenance (snow removal, trash removal, lawn care, pest control) *
- Vacancy Allowance **
- Property Management (if applicable)
- Condo fees (if applicable)

*Jonquil recommended including five to eight per cent of rental income for repairs and maintenance, depending on the condition and type of property and the type of rental, as a safety net for predicting cash flow.

**Jonquil also recommended including five to eight per cent of rental income as a vacancy allowance for multi-unit properties as a safety net for predicting cash flow.

Debt Service:
- 1st Mortgage
- 2nd Mortgage (if applicable)
- Other debt service (if applicable)

Operating Expenses Not Included in Cash Flow Calculations:
- Advertising
- Accounting
- Bookkeeping
- Office expenses (including telephone)
- Supplies
- Legal fees

MORTGAGE REPAYMENT INCREASES EQUITY

"When you have positive cash flow coming in each month," Jenny continued, "your mortgage payment is included in your expenses, so that means your mortgage principal is being reduced and, eventually, will be paid off by your tenants. Each month they are paying you, the owner, for a home to live in and each month you are taking part of that rent and paying your mortgage, which includes principal and interest. Your tenant is reducing your debt and that is increasing your equity each month."

"What do you mean by 'equity'?" questioned Jackie.

Jenny responded by paraphrasing the Wikipedia definition of equity:

In accounting and finance, equity is the difference between the value of the assets, and the cost of the liabilities of something owned. For example, if someone owns a home worth $300,000, but owes $225,000 on that home, they have $75,000 in equity.

"This means that in twenty-five years or less, depending on the term of your mortgage, and whether you make extra payments or remortgage to take out equity, your cash flow will jump. Using the previous example, if your mortgage payment is $939 each month, when that mortgage is paid off, you add $939 to your current $327 cash flow and welcome $1,266 to your monthly income. This money can be available to you earlier if you sell or refinance.

"You can see," said Jenny, "why I get so excited by the idea of investing in real estate!"

Jonquil added, "This is why having even one investment property in your portfolio can make a huge difference to your retirement income." She also cautioned that there are many things to consider before running out and buying an investment property.

APPRECIATION

"The third way to make money with real estate is through appreciation," Jenny said. "However, we were warned in the real estate investment club that you can't count on appreciation as a given."

Housing markets can continue to go up and up, as they did in the 1980's in Canada, and in the early 2000's in the U.S. Then the bubble burst in Canada in 1988 with prices dropping by one third in the larger cities. In 2008 in the U.S., housing prices tumbled by half in the hardest hit cities. In general, the larger the city, the more volatile the prices are. That translates into larger gains, but also larger declines.

Jonquil surprised everyone by telling the group that there are actually two types of appreciation—market appreciation and forced appreciation.

"*Market appreciation* is what Jenny was referring to," said Jonquil, "and is beyond your control. It is based on market prices rising in the face of increasing demand for housing in a specific area. Market appreciation generally follows the laws of supply and demand and requires population growth in that area. In a shrinking market that is losing population, it is rare to have appreciation. Prices tend to fall in these situations, when the supply of housing exceeds demand.

"*Forced appreciation* is a result of adding value by making improvements to the property. This can be from renovations, or management improvements, to an income property. Forced appreciation, unlike market appreciation, is within your control," said Jonquil. "It is the value that you create."

LEVERAGE

"Another key benefit of investing in real estate is leverage," said Jonquil. "You can get a low interest loan secured against your property, in the form of a Line of Credit or Mortgage. On an investment property valued at $300,000, you can secure up to $240,000—that is eighty per cent of the value of the asset!

"If you were buying the property for your personal residence, your mortgage could be up to $285,000, or ninety-five per cent of the value of the home," Jonquil pointed out.

"Another type of loan for an existing property is a refinance," said Jonquil. "Refinancing has the effect of returning capital to the investor and is considered similar to a sale. The proceeds can be used to finance additional purchases, for renovations to stimulate forced appreciation, or for emergency situations."

"If you had a hundred thousand dollars invested in mutual funds, stocks or bonds, a brokerage will allow you to borrow seventy per cent of the value of your portfolio to invest. This is called a 'Margin Account'," said Jonathan. "Any borrowed funds must be used within their brokerage. A big concern with this type of leverage is, if the stock market drops and the value of your investments fall, the borrowed funds can get called in, meaning the brokerage will ask for repayment of their 'loan'."

CONTROL WITH CAUSE

Jenny told everyone about a key strategy that she and her husband had thankfully followed for investing in real estate. "Whenever you purchase a property, you need a clear idea what your exit strategy is going to be," she said. "Never buy a property that you can't sell. Know what sells in that area. This gives you more control."

During their networking, Jenny and her husband had learned of a strategy for beginning investors that provided more control and was also a great exit strategy. It focused on the most popular homes. That translated into homes that are easier to rent and easier to sell.

"We did our research and bought a property with a **CAUSE**," said Jenny.

Convenience: Close to good schools, shopping and transportation

Attraction: Attracts families to that neighbourhood

Under: Is five to ten per cent below the average price for that property type in that city or suburb

Starter: Almost always the most in-demand home and more affordable; facilitates a quicker tenant rental or sale

Economics: Strong fundamentals for growth, stability and rent vs. price, including low vacancy rates

"When we eventually had to sell our home and our investment property because of our pending divorce," Jenny said, "this advice saved us a lot of money and headaches."

Jonquil continued, "If possible, buy properties at a discount to the current market value, so if you decide that it was a mistake to buy the property, or you have to sell, you can turn around and sell quickly and feel secure that you won't lose money. That provides you with more options and, therefore, more control."

Jonathan had been quiet up until now. "These properties with a CAUSE put money in your pockets each and every month. They have more than one exit strategy and they primarily have risks that you can control," he said, "unlike the stock market. Many people believe that tenants are a hassle, so that reduces my competition."

Jonathan then told stories of buying and selling several rental properties, and how he learned by trial and error. He started in his twenties with a single-family home in the U.S. Unfortunately he had to sell it a few years later, because of a marriage breakup. This derailed his retirement plan in many ways and Jonathan did not get back into the real estate market for several years.

His next purchase was a vacation property, where he spent every long weekend and vacation with his new family. Jonathan really enjoyed nature—canoeing, boating and the rocks, water, birds and wildlife. He rented the cottage out in the summer and earned some extra income. As it was not winterized, he could only rent seasonally.

Jonathan needed more support for his retirement than his volatile mutual funds and RRSPs. "Eventually, I started reading books about real estate investing and searching for people that could help me," he said. "I joined a couple of real estate investor groups and started to build a team around me with people that had more experience than I did."

He learned about several success systems, the numbers and contracts. Jonathan discovered and refined a rent-to-own system that he now concentrates on. He also has a few long-term rentals in areas that he expects to have higher than average market appreciation.

Jonquil told the group they would be talking more in depth about the 'how' of investing in real estate including strategies, success systems and numbers the following week. "But first," she said, "we'll take a look at some bigger picture strategies and pitfalls to be aware of."

TIME IN THE MARKET

Napoleon Hill, author of the book, *Think and Grow Rich* said: *'Don't wait! The time will never be just right.'*

Jonquil asked Jenny and Jonathan, "Is it possible to time the market when buying or selling real estate?"

Jenny stated that, in her opinion, real estate has cycles similar to stocks and mutual funds, although the cycles are much longer and, therefore, more predictable.

A prime example of volatile real estate markets is in the oil producing areas. When new oil developments were taking place in Alberta, North Dakota, Oklahoma and Ohio, housing prices rose sharply and the vacancy rate was extremely low. With the fall in oil prices and the rise of renewable energy and climate concerns, these areas are now experiencing sharply lower housing prices and increasing vacancy rates.

Jonathan said that he learned a key lesson with real estate. "It's not when you buy," he said. "It's how long you stay. 'Time in the market' means your tenants are paying down your debt and increasing your equity. Also, the longer you own a rental property, the higher the probability that appreciation will increase its value in your portfolio."

"Let's take a closer look into this most basic and fundamental rule of making money," said Jonquil. "It's true that over the past hundred years, average real estate prices have followed a general upward trend. A rising tide lifts all boats," she smiled.

A deeper look reveals that real estate is an intensely local business. Prices rise and fall as markets go through cycles, and fall into and out of favor. One block can make a difference in supply and demand, and therefore pricing and liquidity.

"Real estate investors need liquidity to be able to make money," said Jonquil.

In this context, liquidity means the ability to easily buy and sell an asset within a short time frame. The degree of liquidity will vary according to the type of asset. In money markets, liquidity is measured in fractions of a second. With real estate, the time scale is much longer, ranging from days to years. The type and location of the property will determine how liquid the asset will be.

Liquidity is also a function of value, risk and price. An overpriced asset will be very difficult to sell, so it will appear to lack liquidity. If you take the same asset and sell it sufficiently below the market price, you may discover a huge line-up of buyers crawling over each other to buy your asset. Liquidity suddenly increases!

Jonquil said, "Many people believe, incorrectly, that real estate isn't liquid. The problem is, most investors and property owners are greedy and are trying to squeeze every last penny out of their property sale."

All professional realtors in Canada and the U.S. list their properties on the Multiple Listing Service (MLS). A closer look reveals that there are several property markets at play simultaneously. Some properties sell very quickly, others take a moderate amount of time to sell, while others seem to be impossible to sell.

"In the period since 2008," Jonquil said, "U.S. real estate markets have been classified as 'buyers markets'. Many markets have experienced huge inventory on the MLS. Properties were taking an average of a hundred and eighty days to sell and, in some markets, they were taking even longer. These market conditions were not very liquid.

"There is a continual ebb and flow to investment," Jonquil went on. "Much of it is predictable if you take the time to observe the trends objectively. Some neighbourhoods come into demand as people move in to take new jobs. Others become desirable because of new amenities like schools, stores and restaurants. Others fall into decay when jobs disappear.

"There is another important, but unspoken, trend in housing. People like to live near people who are similar to them. That is why we see the emergence of ethnic neighbourhoods. Rich people like to live near other rich people. Many cities have a Chinatown, a Little Italy, or a Portuguese district. Once a community gains an identity, it will maintain that identity for a long time. That does not mean things will never change, but if change does take place, it occurs very slowly. Communities develop a reputation that is very difficult to shake."

Jonquil cautioned the group that the next topics were more appropriate for experienced real estate investors with larger projects. However, she wanted to complete her overview of the bigger picture.

FALLING MARKET

Jonquil said that markets can be further characterized by value compared with construction cost. In deeply distressed markets, it is possible to purchase properties below the cost of construction. In some cases, new developments come to a virtual standstill because existing housing is so much less expensive. Where property values are below construction cost, forced appreciation of existing properties is the best way to make money.

In every market, there are some areas that are falling faster than others. Desirable areas can remain desirable, even in a falling market. Prices may fall, but not as fast as the rest of the market. "For example," Jonquil said, "the Phoenix area took a tremendous beating from 2008 to 2011. Prices in the more desirable areas of neighbouring Scottsdale fell too, but not as much."

In times of turbulence, it is often possible to find bargains. A bargain is defined as a property that is at a steep discount to the current market pricing. When you try to sell that same property, will there be buyers? Many investors panic and think that the buyers have all disappeared. Many sellers misunderstand the market. There simply are not as many buyers, and more sellers are competing for fewer buyers. "When there is intense competition, the most competitive sellers will win," said Jonquil.

When a market is falling, many buyers start to look for bargains. They are less willing to pay the market price. If you buy a property at sixty per cent below market value, you can still make a very healthy profit. The key to selling in a distressed market is to price according to the market conditions.

Do not buy property at a ten per cent or even a twenty per cent discount in a falling market. You are almost guaranteed to lose money in that scenario. Transaction costs alone may account for ten per cent of the sale. So you need at least a ten per cent margin just to break even, and a further ten per cent margin to ensure you can sell the property in a reasonable time frame. "There is a phrase that applies here," said Jonathan. "Don't try to catch a falling knife!"

"Imagine if you could purchase a property at fifty per cent below the current market value," Jonquil said. "You could then, immediately turn around and sell it at eighty per cent of the current value, which is twenty per cent below current market prices. By offering a sufficient discount to the market, you can accelerate the sale, still make a tidy profit, and free up the cash to make another deal."

RISING MARKET

In cases where property values are above construction cost, it is possible to find bargains at below construction cost. This enables more extensive renovations to be financially viable. If you purchase highly distressed properties on the edge of good neighbourhoods, these properties are on the wrong side of the street and are associated with a bad neighbourhood. However, by renovating these properties, it is possible to move the line that separates the good from the bad neighbourhood.

Jonquil said, "Prices rise in a market when demand exceeds supply. This is the same for housing as it is for any commodities such as wheat, copper, gold or oranges."

An effective strategy, in these conditions, is to focus on new developments, or the renovation of distressed properties in desirable neighbourhoods. Long-term rentals can also work, provided the ratio of rent to purchase price is appropriate.

Sometimes, in places where prices are rising rapidly, investing in long-term rentals does not work. This is because prices are rising much faster than rents. This happens in very expensive markets where rents remain relatively affordable, even when purchase prices shoot up. This is great for tenants, but not so good for investors.

STABLE MARKET

"A stable market," said Jonquil, "is defined as having relatively stable prices for a period of five years or more. These markets are ideal for long-term rentals. Numbers are easy to analyze. There is a slower, modest population growth and some bargains can be had.

"The focus should be on repositioning properties and bringing them to the highest and best use. In a stable market, there will be better areas available. Buy C properties in a beat-up area, or on the edge of the beat-up area, and reposition them as B properties."

GOOD DEALS GET DONE QUICKLY

Jonathan said, "I've seen properties that sat on the market for a year, and I've seen properties that sold in a few days, with multiple offers. Why do some properties suffer the waiting game, while others seem to be a hot commodity? Location and cycle time play a huge role."

"All good deals get done quickly," said Jonquil. "The question is whether the deal will be done by you, me, or someone else. It will get done. Why? Because, it is obviously a good deal!"

"Great properties are rarely bought below market, and you should only buy great properties," said Jonathan. "Establish what the property is worth to you; then put your best foot forward with a fair offer in order to increase your chance of getting it."

Good deals have a way of being easy to analyze, easy to fund, and difficult to negotiate.

"Think about deals you may have evaluated," said Jonquil, "even your own home. Were they good deals? What did the market tell you?"

Emotion and attachment stand to be the key differences between the purchase of a home that you will live in, and an investment property. "Keep emotion and attachment to the outcome out of real estate decisions," warned Jonquil.

"Wow!" said Jay. "Real estate looks like a smart investment vehicle. But there is so much to learn. I definitely want to know more!"

"That's great," said Jonquil, "because I'm going to go into more detail next week about how to go about investing in real estate. We'll cover specific real estate strategies, success systems and numbers. I want you all to talk to anyone you know that invests in real estate and be prepared to share their stories with the group. See you next week; same time, same place."

Chapter 7:

SUCCESS STRATEGIES

Jonquil shared a powerful quote from Andy Rooney: *'I've learned that opportunities are never lost . . . someone will take the ones you miss.'*

Then she asked, "Who did their homework and talked to people who are investing in real estate?" Jonquil was again surprised when everyone raised their hand. "You guys are keeners!" she said. "Who wants to go first?"

Judit found out that a friend of hers was investing in real estate. Her friend gave her a warning, "A lot of people get into real estate and are not ready for what's about to hit them. Some retreat with their tail between their legs, and some become bitter and tired of presenting their property and managing tenants. Others rush off to find an easier way. They think they must be doing something wrong to make it so difficult, so they take some get-rich-quick type of courses."

Jeff said, "The biggest thing I hear is that they had no idea it could be such a rough ride. Those that pick themselves up and try again are almost always very successful!"

Jordan shared the wisdom from one of his patients, "Problems you can control and fix are opportunities. Problems you can't control or fix are red flags! Beware of the things you can't control or change. Getting a good deal because of a problem isn't really a good deal if that problem is always going to be there, or can't be changed. You are making an investment only if there is a reasonable probability that you will be able to make money when you sell."

Jonathan spoke up, "Some investors have property that makes little sense, considering what they want to achieve. It's what they learned to do from a friend, or a training program they signed up for. Now they are unhappy real estate investors feeling stressed and uncertain. They think they need time management help, or a kick in the butt. What they really need is a plan!"

"I have a dog, named Truffles," shared Jonquil. "She is a chocolate-brown labradoodle, full of energy and curiosity. We go for a walk in the forest and she loves to run. She chases a chipmunk; then a squirrel comes along and she changes direction instantly, and tries to chase both of them at once. If she had focused on the chipmunk, she may have had a chance, but she never did. She was always changing direction and thinking the next squirrel had to be easier to catch.

"Does this sound like your attempt at retirement planning, wealth creation, or real estate investing?" Jonquil asked. "If the answer is 'yes', you are certainly not alone! As humans, we are easily distracted. We are generally lazy, always looking for something more interesting than what is in front of us right now.

"Have you ever been walking down the street, focusing on getting somewhere in record time, only to stop in your tracks when you spot a penny or a dime and are tempted to pick it up?" Jonquil asked.

"We allow low-priority objects or goals to distract us from more important things. We interrupt conversations with family members to comment on silly commercials on TV. We check iPhones and text in the middle of a workout. We allow email to interrupt our activities on the job.

"It's a good idea to consider your options, but don't let them distract you from what's been working for you and helping you achieve your goals. If you have an investing strategy that is working for you, stick to it and master it.

"Most people want to enjoy life," Jonquil continued. "They want time to hang out with their family. As investors, they want to find great deals that will make them money, attract great tenants, and not fall apart after a few months.

"Active real estate investing isn't for everyone," admitted Jonquil. "Active investing in real estate is a business. It is not a hands-off investment. Some people like the idea, but don't have the time to learn the business, or be active in it. Others don't have the money. We'll discuss options for both of these challenges in a couple of weeks."

SUCCESS STRATEGIES

"There are plenty of ways to make money in real estate and we will explore three success strategies. Commercial building strategies will not be discussed," Jonquil explained. "The optimal route is to find a strategy, and get really good at it. Stay focused, become a specialist in your investing area, and you will find your wealth grows very quickly.

"This will be a quick overview with lots of numbers," Jonquil warned. "So hold on and be patient with yourself. I will email the information to you later, so you can concentrate now and not have to take notes. Even if you decide that this isn't your thing, at least you'll have the basics and will be prepared if you ever decide that you do want to invest in real estate, but choose to delegate the day-to-day activities to other investors that specialize in joint ventures or partnerships."

"There are three main success strategies for investing in real estate," said Jonquil. "We'll start with the longest term and end with the shortest term. Buy and hold is obviously for the long term, rent-to-own is a medium-term strategy, and fix and flip is short term."

BUY AND HOLD

"This first strategy is accomplished by purchasing a property and holding that property for the long term, usually several years. Property types can be single-family homes, duplexes, triplexes, four, five, six or seven-plexes, medium and large multi-unit apartments, condominiums and townhouses. Property uses are basically single-family or student rentals.

"Income properties are valued differently than residential real estate. The average value of a single-family home is based on its desirability, features, neighbourhood, location and size. Income properties are valued, based on the numbers. Some areas will have higher rates of return than others. We will use a multi-unit apartment building for our example, since experienced investors often prefer them; mostly because they still have income from the other units if one unit becomes vacant."

Jonquil then wrote a series of terms on the flip chart, discussing each as she wrote them down:

Gross Income = sum of all income sources
"Let's look at the revenue side of the equation first," Jonquil suggested. "You can choose to do this on a monthly, or an annual basis. Be consistent and do not switch back and forth. We'll be doing all of our analysis on an annual basis.

"Add up the rental income from the building. Then add up the revenue from other sources such as parking, laundry and storage. Then subtract provisions for vacancy and maintenance. Depending on the community you are in, this vacancy rate can vary anywhere from one to fifteen per cent. Know the numbers in your community. Gross income equals the sum of all income sources."

Expenses = sum of all expenses
"Now let's look at the expense side of the equation," said Jonquil. "Add together all the expenses associated with the property, including property taxes, insurance, property management,

maintenance, landscape services, snow removal, trash removal and any utilities associated with the common elements for multi-unit buildings.

"Finally, include provisions reserved for unexpected maintenance. This reserve may not get spent on an annual basis, but should be put aside for large expenditures such as replacement of a heating system, redoing a roof or any major repairs. Add this together for the total expenses associated with the property on an annual basis.

"There are a couple of rules of thumb: for single-family homes, the expenses should represent somewhere in the range of thirty to thirty-five per cent of the gross income. For smaller multi-unit buildings, from two to six units, this ratio will increase to approximately forty per cent of the gross revenue. For larger multi-unit buildings, expense ratios can be in the range of fifty to fifty-five per cent of gross revenues, since larger buildings have staff. When you analyze smaller properties, remember that your time also has a value that may affect your return on investment."

Net Operating Income (NOI) = Gross Income - Expenses

"To calculate net operating income (NOI), subtract the total expenses for the property from the gross revenue. Don't include any debt-service related expenses; they get accounted for later."

Cap Rate = NOI/Total Investment

Jonquil continued, "The Cap Rate is, in effect, the base rate of return that the investment will deliver. There may be renovations required to bring the property up to the level where it needs to be, so include the purchase price, plus any renovation costs, in determining the Cap Rate. Divide the net operating income by the total investment in the property, to get the Cap Rate."

Multiples of Net Income = Total Investment/NOI

"Another way to analyze the expenses of a property is to look at multiples of net income. This is almost the same calculation as the cap rate, but in reverse. You divide the total investment by the net income. For example, an eight per cent cap rate would mean that you would be buying a property for 12.5 times the net income. Cap rate is more commonly used and most people understand cap rate."

Cash Flow = NOI – Debt Service
"Net Cash Flow can be obtained by subtracting the debt service (annualized mortgage payments including principal and interest) from the net operating income. You obviously want the cash flow to be positive and lenders for multi-unit buildings will insist upon that."

Debt Coverage Ratio (DCR) = NOI/Debt Service
"The debt coverage ratio is calculated by dividing the positive net income by the debt service. If you have positive cash flow, that will be a large number in the numerator. Most lenders want to see cash flow larger than the debt service by a factor of 1.25 or greater."

TARGET VALUES

"Numbers are important, but you can't go strictly by the numbers," said Jonquil. "For example, the more expensive the property is, the lower the cap rate will be."

In the most affluent areas of major cities, cap rates may be as low as three or four per cent. It is very difficult for a property with a three to four per cent cap rate to deliver positive cash flow with high ratio financing.

Cap rates in less desirable, or more depressed areas, are going to be higher because the cost of acquiring those properties will be much lower when compared with the income. Looking at major cities, you can find cap rates of eight to ten per cent in working-class neighbourhoods.

It is not necessarily a good idea to buy distressed properties in search of higher rates of return. A better way to achieve higher rates of return is by getting a good deal on the acquisition of a property, and buying significantly below its market value. If you are in an area that delivers an eight per cent cap rate as a market average and you buy a property at a significant discount, at a ten per cent cap rate, you know you have a good deal.

RENT TO OWN

This second strategy is accomplished by purchasing a property and renting to a tenant with the option to purchase it within three to four years. You set the purchase price at the beginning, the tenant pays an upfront fee for the option to purchase the home in the future and a portion of their rent is a credit that builds up over time toward their purchase of the home at or before the end of the term.

Rent-to-own is a great addition to a portfolio and has several key advantages:

1. increased cash flow through an up-front option payment, increased rents and lower maintenance expenses
2. a built-in exit strategy through the option to purchase agreement in three to four years
3. a motivated tenant that is proud and responsible for the home

Jonquil noted that rent-to-own generates more cash flow, because the tenants are paying a higher than market rent for their property and they are responsible for basic maintenance. You normally do not need property management, because they are responsible for taking care of repairs up to a certain dollar amount, usually around five hundred dollars.

Jonathan jumped in. "An added benefit is that you're helping people in a big way. Rent-to-own tenants give us warm hugs and handmade thank-you cards, and they invest in fixing up their homes. Regular tenants, on the other hand, rarely mow the lawn!" he exclaimed with a chuckle.

Typical rent-to-own tenants are new to Canada and do not have established credit. Their assets are tied up, they have beaten up their credit because of a health reason, or they just have not saved enough for a full down payment to qualify for financing. Just one setback has knocked their credit down to the point where the banks are not interested. They just need a helping hand, because the banks will not help them, and the other options available do not make financial sense for them.

"There are several possible candidates for rent-to-own," continued Jonathan, "such as doctors and nurses who are moving to Canada, or people going through a divorce, a job loss or an illness. They may have difficulty qualifying for a mortgage. These families are not typical renters. They are more responsible, because they are investing in the home they will purchase in three or four years when their credit is improved or established. They are thrilled to have someone help them get into home ownership!"

Jonquil now took her turn, "There is a great debate around what comes first with rent-to-own—the tenant or the property? No matter which approach you take, screening your tenant is critical —reference checks, employment verification and credit score review.

"You must also make sure the tenants have income levels that will allow them to qualify for financing in the future. You need to review their debt load to make sure the bank is likely to work with them in the future, and you need to review their plan to correct whatever issue they have to make sure they know what steps they have to take to qualify for future financing. Honesty from a prospective rent-to-own tenant is imperative."

Jonquil warned that rent-to-own can get a bad reputation when it is abused by investors who skip the screening process. Some investors are lazy, some do not understand how, or worse, some do it intentionally. They put a tenant in a home knowing the tenant will never be able to buy from them. They take the deposit and the elevated rent and when the tenant cannot buy at the end, they just rent it out again, keeping all the deposits as extra profit. "That is unethical and it is not how rent-to-own should work," said Jonquil.

A) Tenant First

Tenant first is when you have prescreened your tenant. They pass a rigorous screening process, have the income and the deposit, and are ready to go house shopping. Typically you send them out with a trusted real estate agent to look for a home they want to buy. The realtor has your specific criteria for where and what you buy.

The tenant finds their dream home that meets your criteria and you buy it for them. The theory is that they will be more committed to the home, because they have chosen it. These tenants often pay for the home inspection since they selected the home.

A challenge with tenant first is that your realtor must ensure that the tenant only reviews homes that meet your criteria. A family will only be shown homes with a CAUSE, so the home can be rented or sold quickly if something goes wrong.

B) Property First

The property first scenario means you find and buy a property first; then find a tenant who wants to rent-to-own that specific property from you.

A challenge with property first is that sometimes you do not find a tenant quickly. The pool of people who are suited for rent-to-own is a smaller percentage of the rental pool. Sometimes it can take a month or two to fill the rent to own property or you may even find yourself going to a regular rental because the home wasn't attracting a tenant buyer.

To maximize the likelihood that your tenant will succeed and you will make a great return, you need to buy properties for less than the market value. It can be more difficult to do that when a tenant is involved.

Jonathan jumped in, "I'm a real estate investor and love helping people. I make money when I create a great deal. I'm not going to buy a house that doesn't set my tenants up for success, or a house that doesn't have other exit strategies or options."

There are many different variations on the rent-to-own process, but they have one core idea in common: a buyer who does not qualify for mortgage financing rents a home until they qualify; then they purchase the home.

1. Lease Purchase

The tenant buyer signs two contracts. The first is a conventional lease. The second is a traditional agreement of purchase and sale. The closing date is set at the end of the lease. The sale price is set higher than the current market value to take inflation into account. The rent is set above market rent and a portion of that rent is credited to the buyer on closing to assist them with their down payment. This is effectively a form of forced savings that improves the buyer's chances of qualifying for a mortgage loan.

"As an investor, you want to buy below market value, and sell at a higher price that at least keeps up with inflation," said Jonquil.

2. Lease Option

With a lease option, you are providing the buyer with an option to purchase the property at a pre-determined price in the future. They live in the property now as tenants until such time as they exercise the option to purchase the property. This type of transaction is governed by two principal contracts:

1. lease agreement
2. option agreement

"As a landlord," said Jonathan, "you want to minimize the time invested in property management, so it is wise to include terms around maintenance so that only maintenance items above a certain dollar value, often five hundred dollars, will be the responsibility of the landlord. Anything up to that will be the responsibility of the tenant."

The future homeowner will need to be able to maintain the property themselves, and they should treat the property as their own home because it will be in the near future.

The tenant buyer will also have to resolve the issues that are preventing them from securing bank financing on the property now. This could include insufficient credit history, damaged credit, insufficient down payment, or insufficient self-employment income history.

If the buyer has insufficient down payment, they will pay above market rent and a portion of this rent will be credited back to the buyer on closing toward their down payment. This will be detailed in the option agreement. If the tenant fails to exercise the option to purchase, the excess rent is normally kept by the property owner.

The option agreement needs to have financial consideration to make it legal. The option consideration from the tenant buyer to the property owner should be at least four to five per cent of the purchase price. This ensures that the buyer has sufficient financial 'skin in the game' and will not easily walk away from their responsibilities under the agreements.

FIX AND FLIP OR REFINANCE

The third strategy is accomplished by purchasing a distressed income producing property and increasing its value to create forced appreciation. There are then two options, selling the property after the renovations are completed for a short term hold, or refinancing the property based on the increased value from the renovations, and holding it, usually for several years.

Creating value through forced appreciation can be achieved by either renovating the property, or improving the financial performance. This can be accomplished by increasing the rents, reducing expenses through energy savings, installing lower maintenance building products and finishes, and other renovations.

If it is a multi-unit residential property, you can create value by improving the property management. The building may have been running at a fairly high vacancy rate, perhaps thirty per cent, maybe even fifty per cent, below vacancy. You create value by bringing that building up to ninety-five per cent, or even one hundred per cent occupancy.

Once you have created that additional value, then you can refinance the property with a conventional lender and get a seventy-five or eighty per cent loan to value. If you bought it at a sufficient discount, then you can effectively create a no-money-down deal, because you are refinancing at a higher value for the property compared with your original investment.

"Here's an example," Jonquil said. "An apartment building with thirty units is acquired for $600,000. It is distressed and at a fifty per cent vacancy rate. Some of the interiors are old and dated, so you spend $5,000 to renovate each unit ($150,000 in total renovations). That brings the total investment to $750,000.

"The after repair value of this building, once stabilized with a hundred per cent occupancy and slightly higher rents, is now worth possibly $1.2 million. You have created $600,000 of added value over the original $600,000 that you bought the property for.

"You can then go to a commercial lender and refinance the property at seventy-five per cent of $1.2 million after-repair-value so the lender gives you $900,000. Only $750,000 was invested initially ($600,000+ $150,000) and you are getting $900,000 from the lender, so you are holding a property generating positive cash flow with no cash invested in the deal. That's one way to create no-money-down deals in today's market," Jonquil said.

This is a powerful approach and lenders like it too, for a couple of reasons. They feel much more comfortable in financing a building that is seasoned. This means that the property has been under management control for a period of time, perhaps a year to eighteen months. In those eighteen months, you can demonstrate to the lender the performance of the property and your ability to manage the property. You get some history and that lowers the risk significantly in the eyes of the lender.

Jordan asked, "Where do you get the money to acquire the building and renovate it?"

"An excellent approach is to joint venture with funding partners. These are private individuals that have cash sitting in the bank earning very low rates of return. You offer them the opportunity to put up the equity," said Jonquil. "We'll talk about joint ventures and partnering in a couple of weeks."

To finish this example of raising $750,000, you would take a third of that in the form of equity, so you would ask for $250,000 in equity from a private investor. Then you go to a bank that specializes in construction loans and borrow two thirds, in this case $500,000, to complete the purchase and the construction. You are essentially doing a sixty-seven per cent loan to investment with a private lender, then one third of the overall investment with an equity investor. Mortgage brokers can become invaluable resources in helping you develop relationships with both banks and private lenders.

Both the equity investor and the lender are going to be looking for above average rates of return. The construction lender might be looking for a premium over the conventional market. The conventional market premium might be four or five per cent annual interest rate, so the construction lender might be seeking a ten to twelve per cent interest rate. At the end of the day, there are more than enough profits in the deal to pay for that ten to twelve per cent.

"The key here," Jonquil said, "is that it's not the interest rate that matters. It's whether you can make the numbers work, so that the deal generates sufficient profit over a twelve to twenty-four month time horizon for the deal to financially make sense."

There is another kind of no-money-down deal. Many apartment buildings are owned by people approaching retirement age. They may be unsure about their children's ability or desire to own and manage income properties. Some of these buildings have been owned for many years and there is a lot of equity in the property. They may even be owned free and clear or have no debt against them.

When an elderly person is selling a building with the intent to simply cash out, they will face a very large capital gains tax payment. In this case, one approach is to ask the owner for a vendor take-back, which is essentially seller financing. That will enable the seller to continue to enjoy some income from the property without the headache of owning it. The seller would hold a note, or have a mortgage on the property and would enjoy the income without owning the property.

The advantage to the seller, since they have not actually sold the property, is that the capital gains tax bill is not due at that point. They can effectively defer a portion of that tax and gain significant financial advantage by continuing to put that money to work, as opposed to simply giving it to the CRA or IRS.

"This is a way of structuring things for a win-win situation," Jonquil said.

You could see the wheels turning when Jonathan asked, "Can you turn that into a no-money-down deal?"

Jonquil had an answer, "Go to a conventional lender to finance the building and get a reasonable ratio loan, say seventy-five per cent of value. Then go to the owner of the building and get them to write a second mortgage behind a primary commercial lender for the balance of the building. This would be twenty-five per cent, so the seller gets a large cheque on the sale of the building for seventy-five per cent of the money. They leave a quarter of the equity tied up in the property, and will continue to get an income stream from that twenty-five per cent. Their biggest advantage is deferring the tax on the sale of the building because they haven't fully realized the gain.

"From the seller's point of view, they are secure because, if there is a default on the loan, they can simply foreclose and own the building again and are no worse off than before. If the building was a good asset for them in the past, it will still be a good asset even if they are forced to foreclose on it, because the buyer didn't perform on the second mortgage.

"What is the end result?" asked Jonquil. "The seller is secure. The buyer gets a great deal, because they are essentially getting a no-money-down deal, or a potentially very high ratio financing deal. It's a win-win scenario for everyone!"

Real estate investors can be categorized into 'market follower'—often a new investor just starting out or with a few properties already; or 'market maker'—an experienced real estate investor, usually with larger properties.

MARKET FOLLOWER

"A market follower," said Jonquil, "goes into a local real estate market, buys a single home, renovates it, then sells it. They have no control over the after-renovation value of the property as it is determined by the current sales history of comparable properties in the same area. This is classic market following and a game of 'Russian roulette'."

The investor has no long-range plan and simply buys, renovates and hopes to sell at a price higher than their purchase price plus the cost of the renovations. They are not aware of where their specific market is in the real estate cycle. The market may start falling before the renovations are completed. A market follower's fortunes are won or lost by the unpredictability of the market.

MARKET MAKER

"A market maker," said Jonquil, "undertakes a larger vision. They see a business opportunity to satisfy the market opportunity. The bigger the vision, the more you can influence the perceived value of the final product."

Buildings have an intrinsic value based on their bricks, mortar, wood, wiring, and plumbing. This construction cost is the baseline. Anything more than that is the subjective value associated with location.

Jonquil asked, "Why does an apartment in Manhattan sell for fourteen hundred dollars per square foot, when a property of the same size in a rural area sells for seventy dollars per square foot? Is it really worth twenty times more?

"Some large vision projects have missed the market. They are called 'white elephants'. How do you prevent a large project from becoming a white elephant? By conducting proper test marketing, you can gain a sense of the appetite for your proposed product."

Jonquil knew it was time to end this meeting. There were a lot of starry-eyed people in the group and she had covered more than most wanted to know.

"That's it for today," she said, amidst sighs of relief. "Next week we'll talk about focus, location and where to find investment properties. Ask your real estate investor contacts to tell you where they invested and why they chose that area. See you then."

Chapter 8:

REAL ESTATE BASICS

"How many of you think you are good at multi-tasking?" asked Jonquil. About half of the group raised their hand. "Did you know that it leaves you feeling emptier and more disconnected because interactions are more superficial?" she asked, rhetorically.

"Studies show that we are not going to get better at it, and we will never be as good as if we just focused on one thing at a time. When subjects switched back and forth between tasks, total task time took twenty-five per cent longer than if they did one task and moved on to the next."

Judit agreed. "We put more value on the number of activities we're juggling than we do to prioritizing and focusing our activities, which is the real route to creating value that lasts."

Jeremy added, "Beware of the shiny object syndrome! Most days are spent not even being aware that we're shifting focus reactively whenever something new draws our interest. We're failing to make conscious and intentional choices about where to put our attention."

"We face more distractions in our lives than ever before in this digital age," said Jackie. "It's about engaging with full concentration to improve one's performance."

FOCUS

Jonquil found a quote from Tony Schwartz that says: *'You can achieve excellence in almost any domain through single-minded focus and practice. On the other hand, mobilizing sustained, single-minded focus is a difficult, energy-draining, often uncomfortable process and it doesn't come to us naturally. We're hardwired to be alert, vigilant, and quickly attentive to every new potential danger and threat.'*

"Did you learn anything about focus when talking with real estate investors this week?" Jonquil asked.

Jonathan knew some unfocused investors from his investment club that race all over Canada and the U.S. trying to find the perfect investment market. They find it overwhelming trying to pick the perfect market. "It's not about finding the perfect market," Jonathan said. "It's about finding a market with decent fundamentals that will allow you to live life on your terms."

"The idea that you have to find the perfect investment market is ludicrous," said Jonquil. "It doesn't exist. Every single market has positive and negative aspects. Some are better places for capital appreciation. Others are more stable and you make your money on mortgage pay down and cash flow, because you're not going to see values change that much. Some markets are even declining."

Jonquil told the group that her preference was to invest in a market that is stable, with modest growth, where nothing happens too quickly, allowing her time to make careful decisions. "I like a market that doesn't generally shift overnight with massive increases or drops," said Jonquil, "both of which can cause a lot of headaches as an investor."

Jenny jumped in, "When I spoke with people, some were actually ashamed of where they invested, because it wasn't on someone's top ten listing. I think those that should be ashamed are the ones that use that as their main consideration; they awkwardly tried to buy in some top market, just because the property happens to be on a real estate investment group's top ten list. If you like to travel to Vancouver, Phoenix or Florida, are excited about the market, and have a team in that area, and if you want to have distance between you and your investment properties, then go for it."

"You can make money in the hottest markets if you know what you're doing," Jonquil said, "but be prepared to have more competition, and often lower returns on your investment. So, it's not necessarily about the market. It's more about matching your strategy with the market and the real estate cycle that a market is in. Most importantly, it's about making sure you're buying property that fits with your 'why'. I am assuming you have all worked on that collage project I assigned a couple weeks ago, and that it has been helping you determine your 'why'. Your 'why', in all honesty, becomes your single most powerful reason for doing this."

"Once you determine your 'why', you then need to focus on the 'what' and 'how'," said Jonquil. She wanted to get the group focused on the next steps. "The next thing you do," she said, "is you choose a property type, then a market area, then a submarket. You become the known expert investor for that area—then focus on finding great deals."

"What type of residential investment property is best for you?" asked Jonquil. "Let's keep it simple and look at the pros and cons of single family homes, multi-unit family homes and condominiums."

SINGLE FAMILY HOMES

Single family homes are the simplest investment to pursue. Most people have lived in a house, so they can relate to the decisions involved in home selection. It is usually easier to find tenants for a single-family home and also easier to attract a lender to finance the property. Single-family homes generally hold their value much better than other options in the residential market.

"Somebody needs to be responsible for the upkeep of the yard and snow removal," said Jonquil. This is often included in the rental agreement with tenants. However, it is still the investor's responsibility to ensure it gets done.

The challenge that many areas now face in North America, especially in and around larger cities, is that single family homes will not cash flow without a second rental unit. If there is only one unit in the home, it is very challenging to buy the home and have the rent cover the mortgage, maintenance and property management and still put cash in your pocket.

"To make purchases like this work," Jonquil suggested, "you need to buy below the market value; then add a legal suite, or use a rent-to-own program."

Jonquil used the flip chart to compare investing in single-family homes with multi-family homes.

Advantages of Single Family Homes

- Normally appreciate faster than multi-family units
- Generally a broader range of potential buyers
- Often worth more on a per unit basis
- More liquid even in a down market
- Only have to deal with one tenant
- Tenants do not argue with other tenants, because they are the only ones living there
- Easier to get tenants to pay for all of their utility bills
- May get a better quality of tenant
- Financing investor properties is usually simpler and easier to get

Advantages Multi-family Homes

- Potential cash flows are better, because there are more units purchased for a slightly lower price per unit

- More than one renter to help cover operating costs
- Often a larger range of possible tenants
- If one unit becomes vacant, you can work on it and still be collecting rent from other units
- Economies of scale: property management fees are lower per unit
- Utility costs will likely not be three times the amount if it is a three unit home
- On a per unit basis, multi-family homes are less expensive
- Generally, the rent to price ratio is higher and this often equates to more cash flow

Disadvantages of Multi-family Homes

- Limited exit options
- More work to manage the property
- Potential buyers are limited to investors
- Financing may not be available at the bank branch level, so you would not have the leverage from your existing relationships

CONDOMINIUMS (STRATA TITLE)

Condominiums are becoming more common in urban areas as the price of land rises and the cost of living close to the centre of a city becomes prohibitive for the average person. The concept of a condo, in Canada and the U.S., is that you have ownership of your unit and shared ownership of the land and other parts of the building. Strata Title is the common term in Western Canada.

"Many people think of a high-rise building when they hear the word condominium," said Jonquil. "In reality, a detached home can be a condominium just as easily as a unit in a high-rise building. It simply means that the land that the home sits on is a common element."

The unit is owned by the person on title, but everyone shares the cost of ownership for common elements such as walkways, driveways, hallways, lobbies, security, amenities like workout rooms and pools, stairways and electrical systems that are not part of the space that belongs to individual owners. As an investor, you need to be aware of the maintenance fees that are associated with a condo property. You are also paying a management fee on these expenses, unless you self-manage the expenses to save money, or have more control over them.

Jonquil warned, "Be sure you review the condo minutes from past meetings to get a sense of how the building is being managed and any potential issues that may require a special one-time fee charge."

LOCATION, LOCATION

When evaluating market areas, Jonquil listed the following elements on the flip chart:

- familiar area
- population growth
- good employment
- good transportation
- healthy housing economy
- appealing opportunities

"Research all the elements on the checklist," said Jonquil, "and think about prospective tenants. Where will they work? How will they get to work? Where else would they live, if not in the area you're looking at?"

Good location research before you buy a property will increase the likelihood of making a good return from the property. Think about an exit strategy. Buy each property with the end in mind. Before you buy, envision yourself selling.

Investing in an area you already know well reduces your learning curve significantly. Unless the market you are in is shrinking, or is very expensive, you will have an easier time starting if you focus close to home.

"When researching an area," Jonquil said, "there are some key questions that you need to find answers for." She listed them on the flip chart:

1. Is the population growing or at least stable?
2. Is the average income increasing faster than other areas?
3. Is the population aging or is it younger?
4. Is the area economy growing? Is there new construction? Are companies adding jobs?
5. Are the number of schools increasing or decreasing in the area?
6. What is the general sense in the media about the area?

"Notice the trends," Jonquil said, "and continue to ask questions. Over the last five to ten years, have more people been consistently moving into the area than moving out? Where are the new people coming from? What is the health of the housing market? If there is excessive building and expanding housing inventory, is the population expanding enough to keep up? What is available and what is coming up? Why are things up or down? Look at sales to listing ratios, rental rate trends, post price trends and vacancy rates."

Jonquil listed some bigger picture items to watch out for on the flip chart.

Government plans—Changes in tax laws or infrastructure.

Interest rates—What people think is going to happen with interest rates will trigger short-term opportunity.

Development—Is there something preventing development in an area? If so, that is positive in most cases. If businesses and governments are investing in that area despite a lack of new development, it is a very good sign.

Availability of land—This is related to new development, but it is important to look at as you drive around a potential area to spot opportunities.

Real estate cycles—Is the area expanding or contracting? A recent book entitled, *Secrets of the Canadian Real Estate Cycle* is an excellent resource for Canadians.

BECOME A SUBMARKET EXPERT

"What is more important in real estate investing," asked Jonquil, "location or becoming a local expert?" She was proud of the group when they all responded, "Become a local expert!"

A submarket is a small market area that you can walk around in about forty minutes. A promising submarket should have home prices below the city average, but rent rates similar to other, higher-priced areas.

The submarket also needs to be strong in accessibility with quality schools and local jobs. "Look for major transportation hubs, major facilities like a hospital or university, or even government buildings, and shopping," said Jonquil.

Becoming the known expert investor for an area is the secret ingredient that takes your investments to the highest level without having to dedicate all waking hours to finding great deals. Invest the hours into building the foundation, then it does not take much work to stay on top of things in your submarket and spot the moneymaking deals.

To become a submarket expert, you need to see a lot of homes. Some experts told Jonquil that, "you will know a great deal once you've seen a hundred homes."

"That's a daunting number," she admitted, "and I don't think you have to see a hundred homes before you do your first deal."

Over time, the deals will become so obvious that it will be like there is a neon sign saying 'great deal here'. Because you are a submarket expert, you will know exactly what to say in your head when you go to put tenants into your home, and you will rarely find yourself dealing with a vacancy.

Other benefits of getting to know the neighbourhood are finding and hiring trades people, and having neighbours and friends quickly know what deals you are looking for and send them your way. They will tell other people about you, because you have homes in the area.

Creating Deals

"Most great deals are not found, they are created," said Jonquil. "Deals are created through negotiating, solving problems, spotting opportunities and adding value. The easiest way to be able to do this is to become an area expert and mine that area for opportunities.

"Ideally, you want to be in an area where first-time homebuyers like to buy. That will help with your exit strategy when you want to sell in the future. Look for pockets with potential. Find a starving crowd of renters looking for good quality homes and get to know exactly what they are looking for."

Analyzing Deals

Jonquil asked the group, "Do you ever watch 'Dragon's Den' in Canada; or 'Shark Tank' in the U.S.? Both shows are entertaining and educational." About half of the group, mainly those that were older than Jonquil, raised their hand. "Pay attention to the questions of the dragons and sharks, and the observations they make," continued Jonquil.

Kevin O'Leary was on 'Dragon's Den', and is now on 'Shark Tank'. He is the most black and white when it comes to the subject of risk versus reward. Other sharks may invest for reasons beyond risk and reward, but he does not. For him, it is always about making money. He is entertaining, obnoxious and single-minded in his investment strategies.

He often refers to his dollars as soldiers. Kevin sends them off to battle only in the highest likelihood they will win and return with more soldiers. As in any battle, it is inevitable that a few will die, but he wants as many survivors as possible.

"What could happen to cause your soldiers to die at war?" Jonquil asked. "Those are the risks you will be taking. Often, the higher the potential profits and rewards, the higher the risks are that you could lose your money."

Kevin's point is to focus on the end when you start. What is the likelihood that you will get your money back, with a return, at the end?

"Focus is the word, again," said Jonquil, "on a bread-and-butter approach, a basic strategy that's easily repeatable with lower risk resulting in less stress. The returns are good, but not as large as some other riskier strategies, and they take time to materialize."

Estimating Expenses

Most rental properties have expenses of at least thirty-five per cent of the revenue. We have already discussed that expenses include property taxes, house insurance, property management, maintenance, materials, water, sewer and garbage. The remaining sixty to seventy per cent of rental income will pay for financing costs and some cash in your pocket each month.

With rent-to-own, expenses are lower because the tenants are responsible for more of the expenses. About twenty per cent of revenue is more accurate for rent-to-own expenses like house insurance and taxes. You do not need a property manager, you will have less maintenance, and your tenant will normally pay for water, sewer and garbage.

Jonquil summed up, "At some point in your evaluation of a property, you'll have enough information to get a clear picture of whether the prospective property will have a positive cash flow or not. Only invest in properties with a positive cash flow."

REAL ESTATE MARKETS—CANADA VERSUS U.S.

Pierre Elliott Trudeau once said: *'Living next to the U.S., in some ways, is like sleeping with an elephant. No matter how friendly and even-tempered the animal, one is affected by every twitch and grunt.'*

"If you are a Canadian thinking of investing in the U.S., or vice versa," said Jonquil, "it is important to know that there are profound differences. Here is a quick overview, but you can find out more in a very informative book entitled, *The Great Canadian Takeover* that goes into greater detail.

Privacy

"Canadians enjoy a level of privacy that is taken for granted," said Jonquil. "By contrast, in the U.S., there is a vast amount of data that is a matter of public record that anyone can simply find by searching on the Internet." This caught everyone but Jeremy by surprise.

In many counties in the U.S., the County assessor maintains public records of who the official owner of the property is, their personal address, the taxes owing for each year, and whether the taxes are paid up to date and on time. Many counties even include a photograph of the property. To Canadians, this is a shocking level of public disclosure.

The county recorder's office maintains a corresponding level of detail in the title of the property. These records can contain the last sale date of the property, the sale price, and whether there are any liens on the title. All this information is readlly accessible for anyone to see. It is extremely difficult in such an environment for the seller to negotiate. The buyer can estimate how much equity is in the property, and this significantly strengthens the buyers negotiating position.

The MLS System

In Canada, the MLS system and any region is a single database, which all realtors and the general public have access to. The brokers and realtors have a more advanced view into that database called the MLX database.

"By contrast, the MLS systems in the U.S. are much less integrated," said Jonquil. "Not all realtors reveal the complete view of the MLS system to their clients, so finding a property can be far more complex. Some realtor sites only present their own listings."

The analyst databases are also fragmented by area. If you are an investor looking to buy income properties in the U.S., you will find it much more difficult to search multiple databases simultaneously. An integrated view of the MLS on sites such as realtor.com can be much more useful.

Short Sales

Short sales are a foreign concept to Canadians. This occurs when a house is worth less than the market mortgage on the property. A seller can ask the bank permission to sell the property for less than the mortgage value. If the bank agrees, then the sale completes, and the seller has a less severe impact on their credit rating than a foreclosure or bankruptcy.

Lawyer versus Title Company

In Canada, most real estate transactions are closed by lawyers, except in Quebec where a notary can oversee the process. In the U.S., the process varies by state. Some states are attorney close states, and others require only title company oversight.

In Illinois, transactions are closed by title companies, but the documents must be prepared by an attorney. So, attorneys act as agents for the title companies. Other states such as Arizona can fully close the transaction with the title company and no lawyer is required.

Deeds

There are several types of deeds in the U.S. They vary by state and sometimes by county. The most common types of deeds fall into four categories:

- Warranty deeds
- Quit Claim deeds
- Special Warranty deeds
- Tax deeds

Closing Dates

In Canada, the closing date on a firm agreement of purchase and sale is treated like a sure thing. The transaction will almost always close on schedule. The lawyers of both sides will schedule signing meetings a couple of days in advance for each side respectively. On closing day, funds are advanced, documents are recorded, and keys are delivered. "I've never had a late closing in Canada," said Jonquil.

"I haven't either," said Jonathan.

By contrast, closing dates in the U.S. seem to be rescheduled with regularity for numerous reasons. There is even a term for a closing when the funds do not appear. It is called a 'dry close'.

Delays occur because of several reasons:

- Lender has not completed their underwriting process
- Lawyer for one of the parties is too busy, or on vacation

- Required documents and stamps are not ready
- It is not convenient for one of the parties

This disregard for the sanctity of the closing date is often a huge shock to Canadian investors who are not accustomed to this loose way of doing things.

Tax Planning

There are significant differences between the taxation structures in the United States versus those in Canada.

In Canada, there are three basic entity types that are appropriate for holding real estate:

- Federally incorporated corporations
- Provincially incorporated corporations, and
- Limited partnerships

The United States has more types of entities:

- LLC (limited liability company)
- Limited partnership
- C – Corp, and
- S – Corp.

Some of these are appropriate for holding real estate, and others are not. Some entities can have unfavourable tax consequences if they are not set up correctly.

Asset Protection

It is generally accepted that investment real estate is best held in an entity to limit exposure to litigation and protect assets from potential risks. The U.S. is one of the most litigious countries in the world.

Canada U.S. Tax Treaty

The Canada U.S. tax treaty is a complex document with many nuances and special cases. The basic idea is to prevent investors from being taxed twice on the same income, by both the U.S. and Canadian governments.

"It is important to ensure that the structures you choose on both sides of the border fall under the tax treaty, otherwise you will be subject to being taxed twice on the same income," warned Jonquil.

Estate Planning

Canada does not have estate taxes per se. Upon death, the Canada Revenue Agency asserts that there is a deemed disposition. If any assets deemed to be sold at that time have a capital gain associated with them, then the capital gains tax on those assets become due and payable.

If the Canadian assets are held in a corporation, the corporation does not die. The shares held by the shareholder would be subject to the 'deemed disposition' and the capital gains calculation.

The U.S. has estate taxes, and the most onerous estate taxes are generally reserved for foreigners and non-residents. There are structures that Canadians can set up to eliminate this tax obligation.

"If you want to have a winter home, or investment properties in a warmer climate like Florida or Arizona," warned Jonquil, "you'll definitely want to do your due diligence and have a knowledgeable cross-border lawyer and accountant on your team." With that comment, Jonquil wrapped up the week's meeting.

"Now that we've learned even more than some of you wanted to know about hands-on real estate investing, we'll talk about hands-off real estate investing next week. There are done-for-you strategies where you can get the benefits of investing in real estate without the detailed knowledge, or time commitment."

"That's definitely for me," said Jordan.

"Me, too," said Judit.

"This coming week, with all of your new knowledge, think about what is holding you back and what you could use to overcome these hurdles," Jonquil said. "See you soon!"

Chapter 9:

OPTIMIZE YOUR TIME

Robert Kiyosaki, author of *Rich Dad, Poor Dad* said, *'If you want to go somewhere, it is best to find someone who has already been there.'*

"What are some of your concerns regarding investing in real estate?" Jonquil asked the group.

Jordan was very interested in getting into real estate investing and was quick to start off the week's discussion. "Time is my most scarce commodity," he said. "I wouldn't have the time, or want to take the time, to learn what I would need to know to be successful. When I'm away from my dental practice, I want to spend time outdoors with my family, not looking for, or looking after tenants. How can I delegate to achieve the same results?"

Jenny was also quite interested and agreed, "I'm very busy at the hospital and don't want to spend my time researching, negotiating and managing tenants! I want to travel and have someone else look after my investments."

Jeff liked the idea of investing in real estate, but also did not have time. He was away on long haul trips during the week and sometimes over weekends. "I don't have the time to learn how or to find and manage tenants," Jeff said.

Judit was excited about finding somebody else to invest in real estate for her. "We have the money in our savings and RRSPs, but don't have the time to do this on our own. I want to know more about this done-for-you opportunity," she said.

Jeremy, too, was interested, but worked long hours as a manager for his U.S. company. "I now feel more hopeful," he said. "I know I need to get into shape both physically and financially. The income is there, so I need someone to channel it into the right vehicle, so I can eventually retire."

"My key regret," Jonathan said, "is that I didn't try to finance more real estate deals when I was working full-time. If you have a job now and are thinking of leaving it in the future to start a real estate business, try to finance as many properties as you can while you have what the bank perceives to be a 'secure job'. You don't want to run out of funds to do the deals you want to do. Eventually, the banks will say no to your next property purchase, even if you have a good job."

Most of the group had never even thought about, let alone knew anything about investing in real estate. After the last few weeks of discussions, they agreed that it looked attractive from a financial and retirement planning perspective. Real estate provided another alternative to their current diet of low-yielding stocks and mutual funds.

REAL ESTATE MYTHS

"Before you determine whether you prefer hands-on or hands-off real estate investing," said Jonquil, "let's unveil more myths . . . this time the myths of real estate. As we learned with mutual funds, some myths really mess with people's lives, finances and retirement prospects."

Myth #1: Passive Income

"Passive means that you are going to 'do the least to get the most'. That might sound like a great idea, but the problem is that trying to build wealth through passive income is like trying to get fit without working out. It is not going to happen.

"If you buy a property, hire a property manager, then choose to do nothing more than deposit the rent money into your bank account, you are setting yourself up for failure. You cannot 'do nothing' and expect to get positive results.

"Real estate is not a passive investment. It is an active business. Like any successful business, real estate investment requires discipline and process. Management is a discipline and should also follow a consistent process. The process sets expectations and boundaries.

"The landscape is littered with properties that underperform as a result of an absentee, passive landlord," said Jonquil. "Passive income is a myth in real estate, unless you're a joint venture partner in a deal. We'll get to that shortly."

Myth #2: Financial Freedom

"What is financial freedom?" asked Jonquil. "Is it a case of never having to worry about money again?

"Some people project that buying thirty properties providing three hundred dollars per month of positive cash flow will allow them to quit their job. Then they will have financial freedom! Active investing in real estate is not the way to go if you never want to worry about money again.

"More properties become just that, and more properties do not equal more freedom. Even if you have the best team, things will require your attention. When you try to finally relax, you will have a tenant move out on short notice, leaving the property to fix up, the hot water tank open, and the plumber not available.

"Murphy's law says that these situations happen all at once," continued Jonquil. "The saying 'when it rains it pours' was not created because of the weather!

"Beware of online sales pitches and direct mail for 'free real estate seminars that will make you rich'," Jonquil added. "The students are told wonderful stories of people becoming rich in a short period of time through hard work and, of course, following the systems that are taught in their weekend seminar, or through courses that will cost thousands of dollars.

"Great things are possible and exceptions happen, but they are not the norm. If you do it on your own, it is going to be a lot more work than you think and take longer than you estimate."

Myth #3: More Knowledge

"Often, the blunt truth," said Jonquil, "is that you don't need another course, or book. You just lack confidence and don't have enough faith in yourself to just do it. If you are missing something, go out and get the information and take action. We'll talk about taking action in a couple of weeks.

"Real estate investing can be scary, but it is also forgiving. You do not have to be perfect in order to make money. However, you never make any money sitting on the sidelines."

Myth #4: Luck

"Have you heard people say that a successful person has been lucky?" asked Jonquil. "That discounts all the time, effort and energy they put into getting to where they are today. It may look like luck, but it is far beyond luck. Those people worked hard, made some tough decisions and persevered when things went wrong.

"Usually the reason that someone says these things is they have completely discounted their own strengths and abilities, and excuse themselves from not achieving success. They blame something else in their lives for the reason they are not the person they want to be."

Myth #5: If They Can, I Can

"This may be true; however, your comparison is usually based on limited information," Jonquil stated. "Your point of reference is whether you can answer these questions about them: How long have they been doing what they do? How big is their team? What sacrifices did they make to do this? How is their health and how are their relationships? Are they happy?

"You probably cannot answer any of these questions and, if you could, you may not want to do what they did at all. Their life may look nothing like what you want your life to be. Just because somebody has ten rental properties doesn't mean they're making money!" Jonquil cautioned.

Myth #6: Perfect Team

"Some people try investing in real estate themselves and get hung up on building the perfect team before they even purchase a property. They spend a lot of time putting together this 'perfect team,' with a good lawyer, property inspector, realtor, mortgage broker and accountant. They are focused on the wrong thing," said Jonquil.

"The team will come and go. Some people will leave the industry for something else, or leave the area for other opportunities. If your intent is to invest in real estate directly, find the people you need, when you need them, and always be on the lookout for new team members."

DONE-FOR-YOU PASSIVE INVESTING

Real estate can be passive, and very lucrative, but someone on your team has to be active. The only way it can be passive is if you work with an active investor who oversees the property from acquisition, to tenant selection, to tenant and property management and everything in between.

Time is scarce. Most people want a more predictable investment vehicle with higher returns, but do not know what to do. They are so busy with their lives they have no time to look and, truth be told, do not know where to look. There is more to do and pay attention to every day. Some find it difficult to even get enough sleep with their work and family commitments. They have no time to get together with friends.

"I hear this from our group," said Jonquil. "How could I possibly add on another activity like investing in real estate, or even researching how to do it? But," she added, "I am here to tell you there is a way. Find an active real estate investor who works with passive joint venture partners. This is the 'Done-for-You' system. You'll spend some time at the beginning of the relationship doing due diligence, some paperwork and signing a cheque. But, once that's completed, it is really passive and done-for-you."

Jay looked up 'Joint Venture' on his iPad and read the definition from Investopedia to the group:

> *A joint venture (JV) is a business arrangement in which two or more parties agree to pool their resources for the purpose of accomplishing a specific task. A JV represents a great way to pool capital, expertise and time, while reducing the exposure of risk to all involved. The venture is its own entity, separate and apart from the participants' other business interests.*
>
> *The task can be a new project or any other business activity. There are many ways to structure a JV. In some joint ventures, each of the participants is responsible for profits, losses and costs associated with it. Other agreements have specific roles and compensation.*
>
> *Many people that have paid off their homes are looking for investment opportunities and are willing to put a line of credit on their property, then loan that money out for a premium. With GIC's and savings accounts making less than two per cent, and stocks and mutual funds being so*

volatile, more and more people are willing to loan out cash for a great return—backed by a cash flowing asset.

"Some joint venture partners make over ten per cent each and every year on their money," said Jonquil. "That is much more than they make on the majority of their other investments, and they can do it without learning the intricacies of real estate or ever handling a troubled tenant call! If you have money to invest and can qualify for financing at the bank, you are in a good position to find someone with the expertise and experience to manage your investment."

JOINT VENTURE SUCCESS

Jonquil asked everyone, "Take note of four keys to creating and maintaining a successful joint venture. They will increase the likelihood of joint venture success and protecting relationships, and apply whether you are the passive investor, or the active investor."

1. Good Fit

Do your research! Find out what is most important to each person. Is there alignment? Is everyone bringing something of value to the table? If there is a fit, then there can be long-term compatibility. When investors bring complementary services to the joint venture and are on the same page about activities, responsibilities and roles, then everything will flow smoother.

2. Roles and Responsibilities in Writing

In any company, roles, responsibilities and compensation have to be clear and fair, or there can be hard feelings. With joint ventures it is no different. Roles, responsibilities and compensation must be in writing, preferably using agreements drafted by an attorney.

3. Business is Business

Treat the relationship like a business relationship. In business, a commitment is a commitment, and it has to be the same when it involves friends or family.

4. Communication is Critical

Do not assume that you know what someone is thinking just because you have known them all your life. Ask for each person's point of view and listen. Watch for nonverbal cues that someone is holding back. Focus on one issue at a time and make sure expectations and plans are clearly articulated before moving onto other issues. Write everything down for best results.

DRIVER OR PASSENGER

There are several ways that joint venture partners can work with real estate investors. If you are looking for passive real estate investment opportunities, you have to first clarify three things: how passive (hands-off), or active (hands-on) you want to be, how much time you have to dedicate, and how much knowledge and experience you bring to the table.

An active investor is the 'driver' of the bus, project, or deal. A passive investor is the 'passenger' on the bus. The art of a successful joint venture is to match your expectations with your partner's passenger, or driver, expectations. Two drivers on one bus can be traumatic!

Passive

"I hear many of you complaining about time pressures and not having enough time to get everything done, let alone add something else like real estate investing to your plate," said Jonquil. "If this is you, then you'll probably want to be a truly hands-off passive 'passenger' and delegate all management decisions to the active and knowledgeable investor; that is, of course, once you agree to the roles, responsibilities and compensation and have them in writing.

"There are two main ways that you can profit from being a totally passive investor," said Jonquil. "We'll touch on them now, but will talk more about these opportunities next week."

1. **HELOC Investor**—"The HELOC (Home Equity Line of Credit) investor will invest funds obtained from equity in their own home. Their funds will normally be invested for a three or four-year term in a rent-to-own project. This investor will be paid a flat service fee, usually at the end of the term for an increased rate of return. They are not responsible for any out-of-pocket expenses such as maintenance and repairs for the project. Their principal will be returned at the end of the term or can be reinvested, at their option, in another project."

2. **RRSP Investor**—"The RRSP (Registered Retirement Savings Plan) investor will qualify for, and hold, a second mortgage on the investment property within a self-directed RRSP at arm's length. They will be responsible for costs to set up and transfer funds to a self-directed RRSP. Their funds will be invested for a three or four-year term that coincides with the first mortgage on the project. This investor will earn interest at an attractive rate of return on their invested funds, of which three per cent will be paid annually, with the balance paid out at the end of the term. They are not responsible for any out-of-pocket expenses such as maintenance and repairs for the project. Their RRSP funds will be returned as cash at the end of the term, or they can be reinvested, at their option, in another project.

"To find out more about real estate joint ventures and opportunities for passive investors," Jonquil said, go to **theretirementcrisis.com**, and review **Online Tool #10**."

Of course, Jay looked it up immediately on his iPad and Jonquil had to bring him back to the discussion in the room.

Partially Active

"Some of you may want to be involved in the initial decision-making regarding the type and length of a project and some on-going decisions, but not the day-to-day activities and responsibilities. You also want the possibility of a higher financial reward and accept the responsibility of higher risk.

"This joint venture," explained Jonquil, "usually involves a sharing of the initial investment, profits and expenses. The split can be anywhere from 50/50 to 80/20, depending on what each party brings to the table and what each party agrees to.

"As a partially active investor, you receive your portion of rent, are responsible for your portion of any out-of-pocket expenses such as maintenance and repairs, and split any profit upon the sale of the property. With this arrangement, you share all of the risks with the active investor—so profit is not guaranteed and an influx of cash may be required at any time for emergencies. The active investor will report on the project, on a monthly or quarterly basis."

Active

"It is very common for active real estate investors with multiple properties to hit a ceiling, where a conventional lender will no longer be willing to lend more money. This is because the higher concentration of debt lies with a single individual. The debt-service ratio is considered too high. In this case, they would have to find other sources of funding, such as private investors or private lenders. They can choose to enter into joint ventures with passive, partially active, or active investors.

"If both investors are active," said Jonquil, "it is even more critical to review the four keys to a successful joint venture, since you will both be 'drivers', instead of a 'driver' and a 'passenger' in this joint venture."

"That happened to me," said Jonathan. "I didn't qualify for the mortgage on a property that I was trying to purchase, so I looked for a joint venture partner. The person that put his hand up was also an active investor, so our negotiations were more 'interesting' than I expected. Everything worked out in the end. It certainly opened my eyes to the importance of partners that complement each other, and that also extends to teams."

TEAM BUSINESS

Jonquil found this quote from Ray Kroc, founder of McDonalds Corporation: *'None of us is as good as all of us.'*

"The key to managing any project is getting the right team. The team is far more important than the deal. A good deal badly managed is no deal. Having the right team is therefore a prerequisite to finding good deals."

Jonathan knew from experience that just hiring the right property manager did not turn real estate into a passive investment. "The property is an object and can't be managed. It's the people connected to the property that need to be managed," he said.

Anyone that is involved with the property—the realtor, insurance agent, property manager, cleaner, lawyer and accountant—needs to be managed. A business that requires management of this many players is an active business.

There are a few key relationships that are critical: mortgage broker, accountant, and attorney. "By maintaining control over the borrower relationship, the financial relationship and the legal relationship," said Jonquil, "you minimize the risk of errors and fraud and ensure that you remain protected."

Systems and Processes

When Ray Kroc bought the McDonald's business from the McDonald brothers in 1961, he did not focus on how to make a hamburger. He focused on the systems and processes required to scale the company to a global business that serves billions of people. These systems are so strong that a teenager can manage an operation that brings in millions of dollars in revenue each year.

All successful businesses require systems to manage situations in a clear and consistent manner. The ability for any business to scale up is limited by the ability to manage exceptions. They usually require the involvement of senior management to analyze the problem and make a decision. If too many aspects of the business require senior management involvement, the business quickly slows to a crawl as there are not enough hours in the day to be involved in so many decisions.

Processes bring consistency and consistency brings quality. Processes create a clear definition of the 'normal' standard, or expected case. They also define when an exception occurs that requires management involvement. By having a consistent outcome, it is possible to minimize exceptions and the resulting management involvement.

Five F System

The Five F system is how you construct your team and system, so that you can focus on your area of specialization and **S**ave **Y**our **S**elf **T**ime, **E**nergy and **M**oney. Ensure that you build a competent team around you so that all the functional areas in your business are operating optimally.

If your strength is marketing, you build the other team members around your marketing ability. If you are a skilled tradesman, you build a team around that competency. Once your team is in place, you and your team execute the Five F system:

1. Find—You research and find a property. It may come from any number of different sources.

2. Figure—You do your due diligence and analyze the numbers for any deal. The key is to make sure that the numbers work, so that any costs associated with acquiring funds can be supported by the overall project. The deal is not a deal unless the numbers work.

3. Fund—You need to raise the funds to purchase the property and fund any renovation work. You could use a combination of debt, borrowing from a lender, and equity, borrowing from a joint venture partner. Lending criteria will vary depending on type of property, community, amount of renovation and your personal situation as an active real estate investor.

4. Fix—You may need to renovate and decorate to get the property into move-in condition. A lot of people enter the business with a background in construction or renovation, so this is where the majority of the money and effort gets invested. They need to ensure that finding, figuring and funding are all covered by other members on their team.

5. Flip or Finance—This depends on your exit strategy. If your exit strategy is to sell the property, then fix and flip it as quickly as possible. If you prefer a long-term hold, then finance it. A long-term hold will be leased to long-term tenants and funded by long-term financing from a bank or commercial lender. This is a partial exit because most of the initial investor capital will be returned in the financing process.

ATTRACTING INVESTORS

"If you're an active investor," said Jonquil, "you may want to attract other investors. If you are quite active, you will eventually need to attract other investors." She wrote down a few suggestions:

1. Area Expert

In most professions, including doctors, car mechanics, computer programmers and accountants, the more specialized you are, the more money you will make. This is the same for real estate investors. The exact same home one street over can be worth $50,000 more simply because of a water view, or some other desirable feature. Real estate is a very local business, so become the area expert.

2. Get Social

Creating a presence on social media platforms such as Twitter, Facebook, Instagram, YouTube and LinkedIn takes time, effort and persistence, just like successful real estate investing.

Some keys to creating positive relationships with social media are:

- Be yourself—tell your own story
- Add value—focus on helping and supporting other people
- Reach out—create conversations, do not just talk about yourself
- Go off-line—have phone conversations or meet at local events

3. Blog, Newsletter, Video

This does not give you instant credibility, but over time as you establish a presence, grow your audience, and share more stories, photos and videos, your credibility can grow exponentially.

4. Press Release

Press releases are under-utilized by most real estate investors. A story that has local appeal, market relevance and a unique angle can create a lot of media buzz.

5. Networking

Involvement in local real estate, investment club and Chamber of Commerce meetings can increase your networking ability and contacts for future opportunities. Support your club by promoting, speaking, or offering introductions to speakers you know.

6. Speaking

When you are a speaker, people find out about your objectives, credibility and interests. They will approach you instead of you having to approach them. Stand out from the crowd and let your expertise show. When there is an opportunity to introduce yourself, speak up and share what you are working on.

7. Book

Publishing a book can give you instant credibility. People learn about your knowledge, experience, interests and passions and that all creates credibility. They will approach you for more information, advice and assistance. The media continually needs interesting and informative content for print, radio and television, and they may request interviews with you.

Jonquil was so excited that she did not realize the time. "Wow!" she said, "Can you tell that I love this topic! It's close to my heart and I enjoy sharing the knowledge that I've learned from the experienced team that I'm putting together."

It was obvious that Jordan and Judit were just as excited as Jonquil was. Even Jonathan learned some new tips to expand his real estate portfolio.

"This week we addressed the concern, 'I Have No Time' by reviewing options to optimize your time. If you decide to go the passive route, remember to go to **theretirementcrisis.com**, and review **Online Tool #10** to learn more about the done-for-you system for hands-off real estate investing."

"Next week we'll deal with the excuse, 'I Have No Money'. You will learn about options to maximize your savings, no matter how much or how little you have. Please talk to your real estate investor contacts," requested Jonquil, "and ask them how they do deals if they have no available cash, or are at their limit with the bank."

Jonquil knew that next week's discussion would definitely boost the hopes of some of the group members.

Chapter 10:

MAXIMIZE YOUR SAVINGS

Jonquil asked the group, "What did you learn in your investigations this week about investing in real estate when you have no available cash?"

Jeff had been on a couple of short haul trips the past week. Since he was home at night, he was able to talk to his neighbour who owns a few rental properties in their neighbourhood.

"I found out that my neighbour started buying properties using the equity in his home and RRSP savings from his friends. He would scout out a bargain house; then talk to his friends to see if they were interested in joining him to purchase it. Sometimes, it took two or three friends to combine their RRSPs to raise enough money for the purchase. I didn't get into the details about how everyone made money."

HIDDEN ASSETS

"Good for you, Jeff!" said Jonquil. "You uncovered two hidden assets for raising equity to provide cash for investing in properties. Jeremy, you will have to bear with us this week since we'll be talking primarily about strategies for Canadians. I don't have the details for the U.S., but I'm sure there are similar strategies to uncover hidden assets there also."

Jackie and Judit both talked to friends that had used equity in their homes to buy a rental property. "I had never heard of this before," said Judit. "This is very encouraging!"

Jackie nodded in agreement. "This would allow my husband and I to get into the real estate game. Who would have thought!" she exclaimed.

"I've done that before," said Jonathan "and it works great! Most people think they don't have any money to invest in real estate. If you own a home, you can investigate arranging for a home equity line of credit on your personal residence. Most banks will look at providing a line of credit secured by your home up to a loan-to-value of eighty per cent.

"What you do is go to your bank and ask them for a home equity line of credit with your home as the backing. The bank registers it on your title that essentially becomes a first mortgage. They call it a line of credit (LOC) or home equity line of credit (HELOC), instead of a first mortgage, but it is essentially the same thing. It is registered against your property in first position.

"Depending upon the value of your home, you may be able to find another investor who has, say $30,000, and is willing to lend their money against your property up to a ninety per cent loan to value. They would register a second mortgage behind the home equity line of credit."

REGISTERED SAVINGS VEHICLES

"There's a very powerful 'Retirement Secret' that we'll talk about in a few minutes," said Jonquil. "Before we do, let's review some of the registered savings vehicles available to us."

The RRSP (Registered Retirement Savings Plan) is the most common retirement account in Canada. Almost every Canadian that earns income in Canada is eligible to have an RRSP. It is not an investment itself, but a vehicle where you can hold investments such as stocks, bonds or mutual funds. It is a special type of bank account that is registered as a trust account with the Canada Revenue Agency (CRA).

Other countries have similar types of registered accounts. In the United States, their version of the RRSP is the Individual Retirement Account (IRA). American corporations offer a 401k to their employees. Australia has a 'super', short for Superannuation, and the United Kingdom has an Individual Savings Account (ISA).

RRSPs and **RESPs (Registered Education Savings Plans)** are among the very few tax breaks that Canadians can enjoy. "When used properly," said Jonquil, "they provide a unique opportunity to build wealth while deferring taxes. However, when misunderstood or used incorrectly, they can make a poor investment much worse!

"The amount that you are allowed to contribute each year depends on your income. Any contributions can be deducted against your personal income. Therefore, the higher your income bracket, the more beneficial RRSPs become."

Jordan agreed. He said he was able to contribute the maximum to his RRSP for a number of years and had built up a substantial savings. He admitted he also used the RESP, designed for parents to save money for their children's post-secondary education. As with RRSPs, gains incurred on investments inside the RESP are tax-free. However, you do not get a tax deduction when you contribute funds to an RESP. There is no annual contribution maximum and your total contribution is limited to $50,000 per child.

The TFSA (Tax-Free Savings Account) is a relatively new type of registered account that the Canadian government introduced in 2009. Any Canadian over the age of 18 can open a TFSA and contribute up to $5,000 per calendar year. The annual contribution limit was raised to $5,500 in 2013, to $10,000 in April 2015, and rolled back to $5,500 in January 2016. Contributions made to a TFSA are not tax deductible against your personal income. The benefit is when you take money out of your TFSA; any gains you made inside the TFSA are not taxable.

The LIRA (Locked-In Retirement Account) and **LRSP (Locked-In Retirement Savings Plan)** are similar and both are designed to hold locked-in pension funds from former plan members, former spouses or common-law partners, spouses or partners that are surviving. The term locked-in refers to the fact that these accounts cannot be cashed out at any time like RRSPs can. These investment funds cannot be removed until certain conditions are met, which are based on the province where the original pension was registered.

Most provinces refer to them as LIRAs. BC, Nova Scotia, PEI, Northwest Territories, Nunavut and Yukon refer to them as LRSPs.

RRIF Surprise

The RRIF (Registered Retirement Income Fund) is a tax-deferred retirement plan similar to the RRSP. The main difference is that the RRIF is not designed to be a savings account like the other registered accounts. Its purpose is to generate income, as opposed to saving money.

Before the end of the year in which you turn seventy-one, it is mandatory to either withdraw all the funds from your RRSP account and pay tax on the full amount, or preferably convert them to a RRIF, or a life annuity. Nobody in the group was at that stage yet. Jeff, the closest to that scenario, was five years away from having to do so.

There are two key differences between a RRSP and RRIF:

1. You are not allowed to contribute any more to a RRIF
2. There is a minimum withdrawal percentage requirement, depending on your age and the total value of the plan. You can choose to take a higher amount than you have to, but you will be taxed on it.

Unfortunately, the idea sounds better than it is in reality. For many Canadians who were counting on the income from their RRIF to support them in later years, the market meltdown in 2008 wiped out much of that retirement income.

Some in the group wondered why the government forces you to begin withdrawing your savings when you turn seventy-one. Jonquil had an answer, "Since your assets have been compounding without the impact of tax, both you and the government hope that you have been able to grow a large nest egg. Now it is the government's turn to take their share of it. They are happy to let you do the hard work of growing your assets tax-free, so they can take a piece of a much larger asset base."

The government knows that it needs to have tax revenue to pay its bills in the future. So the government figured that as long as it starts recovering tax revenues from you in the future, everything will work out. There will be plenty of citizens turning seventy-one each year to help generate tax payments.

"The entire registered account concept is essentially a future savings account for the Canadian government itself," said Jonquil. "That is what I call a 'RRIF Surprise'."

Everyone in the group had their mouths open in disbelief.

Jonquil continued, "In Canada, we have a progressive tax system which means that the more money you make, the higher the tax rate becomes at those higher levels.

"When the government pays you a refund after you paid your taxes and filed your tax return, getting any money back just means that you've been lending money to the government tax-free. You have basically, been overpaying your taxes, so it is your own money that they're giving back to you. They borrowed it from you and didn't have to pay you any interest!"

Most of the group, except for Jay, knew of this concept and tried to minimize their tax refunds for those very reasons.

"Let's look at how taxes affect the advantages and disadvantages of RRSPs," said Jonquil.

RRSP Advantages

Time—The longer you can leave your assets inside an RRSP, the longer they are going to grow without the reducing effects of tax.

Flexibility—Most people do not understand that once your assets are inside a RRSP, you can move the assets around inside without triggering any tax consequence.

Forced Savings—The whole purpose of a registered account is to keep you away from your own money. When the account is registered, the government puts a third party in charge of your money so you cannot access it directly.

Interest Income—Typically taxed at a higher rate, inside an RRSP, all income is taxed at the same lower rate so there is an advantage to having interest income inside your RRSP.

RRSP Disadvantages

Losses—Perhaps the most important downside is that you cannot write off losses incurred in a registered account. During the market crash of 2008, many investors lost fifty per cent of their portfolio value. An account worth $300,000 went down to $150,000. The painful lesson was that $150,000 loss could not be written off against their income to help offset the loss. This is how many Canadians are finding out the hard way they really did not understand their RRSP accounts.

If they had invested in stocks outside their RRSPs, at least they would have been able to write off that $150,000 loss against other investment income they had generated.

"This is a crucial distinction that most investors don't understand," said Jonquil.

Stocks—They normally qualify for a capital gain, but you lose the benefit of the fifty per cent exemption on the capital gain. This is because you cannot claim it as a capital gain inside your RRSP when you take it out.

Dividends—You lose your dividend credit tax credit.

Jordan knew that the key for RRSPs was to invest in types of investments that have minimal risk of losing value. "It's great to be in a position where you don't have any losses in your RRSP," said Jordan. "That's what your goal should be."

RRSP Accounts

"There are two types of RRSP accounts," said Jonquil.

Managed Account—A broker, advisor, planner or asset manager manages the account and contents for you. You are charged directly every time something is bought, or sold, in your account and you may pay a percentage of any profits you make.

Self-directed Account —You manage or direct this account yourself so you do not pay commissions to anyone for making decisions. Since no one else is involved, there is no one else to pay, except for minor administration fees for maintaining the account.

Jonquil said, "A key reason that I reviewed registered savings accounts was to show you how, with some information and effort, you can take control of your finances and do a much better job than someone else will do." The group appreciated her review of registered accounts.

RETIREMENT SECRET

"This also leads us right into the 'Retirement Secret'," said Jonquil. "It could be the single most powerful investment strategy for RRSPs, RESPs, TFSAs, RRIFs and LIRAs. You can even use this strategy outside an RRSP, but doing it within an RRSP provides you with the ultimate power and control.

"Most people believe that mutual funds and stocks are the only investments that are RRSP eligible. They don't realize that mortgages can be held in a self-directed RRSP, RESP, LIRA, or RRIF account."

Jonquil revealed, "This is probably the largest untapped source of funds available to real estate investors, because few people know this option even exists."

Jonquil certainly had the group's attention as she went to the flip chart and unveiled the powerful benefits of the 'Retirement Secret':

1. One of the most stable and predictable investments you can make
2. Consistently produces double-digit returns without significant risk
3. You control how much risk you take
4. No commissions or high fees to advisors or experts
5. Virtually immune to stock market volatility, whether up or down
6. One hundred per cent eligible for RRSP, RESP, RRIF, TFSA and LIRA investing
7. Utilizes a simple, familiar financial product—a mortgage

"The financial industry wants to keep this 'Retirement Secret' a secret," Jonquil disclosed. "Mortgage lending is one of the oldest wealth creation strategies in the financial world, but it has been kept secret by those who understand how powerful and profitable it can be.

"Why do you think the big banks rely on mortgage lending as their bread-and-butter business . . . because it's so profitable!" exclaimed Jonquil. "Canadian banks lend billions of dollars every year on mortgages, because they know that mortgage lending is a very safe and secure way of investing as long as they mitigate their risk.

"Have you noticed that interest rates on mortgages are lower than any other kind of loan you can get?" asked Jonquil. "That's because the banks realize that mortgages are the lowest-risk loan that they offer. Banks don't tell you that one of the eligible investments for a registered account is a 'debt obligation' that includes mortgages! They have no interest in telling you about this, because there's no commission paid to them when you lend money against a mortgage.

"That's why this concept remains a 'Retirement Secret', a little-known investment strategy that you can use with your RRSP and other registered accounts that very few people are aware of.

"Let's review the mortgage basics," said Jonquil. "A mortgage is simply a loan secured against real estate that is provided by a lender to a borrower. You borrow money from a lender to purchase a property, and the lender registers a mortgage on your title to that property to protect their interest. If you stop making mortgage payments, the lender will start the process of taking your property back through foreclosure, then sell the property to recoup their money.

"As a mortgage investor, the most important thing to be aware of is the underlying value of the property, because that is going to be the primary way you protect yourself when you lend money to someone on a mortgage."

Arm's Length Mortgage

"There are specific rules around using RRSP funds for mortgages," said Jonquil. "You can't use non-arm's length RRSPs to fund your investments; that means utilizing funds from your immediate family—spouse, brother, sister, or parents. They need to be arm's length.

"The CRA doesn't want you to loan money to people who are related to you, because they know that you're not always going to keep the loan agreement commercially reasonable. It is intended to be an independent, third-party mortgage, not a financial transaction between two parties that are related. You also can't use RRSP funds for a down payment directly on the same property you are borrowing against. You need to secure the RRSP funds on one property as a first or second mortgage. Then you can use those funds as a down payment on a new investment property."

"Another option that I used," said Jonathan, "is to use your own down payment funds. Then the RRSP funds from your arm's length private lender can hold a mortgage on that property—with no bank needed!"

One of the advantages of using arm's length mortgages, especially with an RRSP, is that by law, the documents have to be set up properly and recorded in order for the mortgage to be an eligible investment in your RRSP. Essentially, you are forced to document the loan properly, so that it meets the requirements of the Income Tax Act.

When an RRSP holder has their funds invested in a mortgage, they do not have to pay management fees, or advisor commissions. They can make a stable and predictable six per cent to ten per cent, or more, return on their money inside their RRSP.

"That certainly is very attractive," said Jordan.

A debt obligation in your RRSP allows you to have a lot more control over risk, you have a say in your return, and you actually have some recourse of action if you are not making the returns that were promised.

"Ask your mutual fund advisor or stockbroker what recourse you have when those funds or stocks you hold with them, go down in value, or disappear altogether," suggested Jonquil.

"This is the most powerful strategy in your investment toolbox," said Jonquil. "Busy people love this option and they can get into real estate without the hassles of being a landlord."

"That's for me," said Jordan.

"Me, too!" agreed Jenny, echoed by Judit and Jay.

"I'm already using it," said Jonathan.

First and Second Mortgages

The terms 'first' and 'second' mortgage refer to the priority they hold in terms of security. A first mortgage is a more secure mortgage on the property, simply because if something goes wrong then the first mortgage holder has a preferred right to try to get their money back. Contrary to what many believe, this does not necessarily mean that second mortgages are risky, as long as you understand how they work and know how to manage your risk.

RRSP Mortgage Lender Benefits

"An investor looking for better returns and alternative investments who has $30,000, $50,000, $100,000, or more, in their RRSP account will be surprised to find all the benefits of an RRSP self-directed mortgage," said Jonquil. "Let's look at how becoming a lender could benefit someone saving for retirement."

1. Passive investment—This is as close to a hands-off passive investment as you are going to find because of the way that a mortgage is set up. The payments from the borrower automatically go back into your RRSP account. They are deducted and withdrawn from the borrower's bank account every month, or every quarter, by the trustee. You do not have anything to do at all once the transaction is set up. Eventually, the mortgage matures and you get your money back. Many lenders do not want their principal back and simply continue on with another done-for-you passive investment.

2. Contribution room maintained—The monthly payments are not contributions to your RRSP; they are returns, so your contribution room is not affected.

3. Double-digit returns—You get double-digit returns with a very simple strategy. Getting double-digit returns is a huge benefit to a lot of investors who hold RRSP accounts because they are scared and do not know how they can possibly make double-digit returns without taking big risks.

"No matter who you are, the stock market is a very risky place to have your money," said Jonquil, "especially if, like most investors, you don't understand what you're doing."

4. Security—The investment is secured by real estate, a hard asset. It is not like putting your RRSPs into the stock market and hoping and praying that those stocks go up. You are getting a defined interest rate with a hard asset backing it up.

5. Consistency—You can make money consistently, no matter what kind of market you find yourself in. This is a very powerful place to be. As long as you do your research properly, you are not taking a big risk. You can make money even when everyone around you is losing forty or fifty per cent on their investments—like what happened to most people in the last few years.

6. Lack of commissions—There are no commissions paid to the financial industry for setting them up. This cuts out the middleman and allows the RRSP lender to make more money, because there is no one standing over you taking a cut of all the investments that you make.

7. Lender rules—"Whoever has the gold makes the rules!" said Jonquil. "When you become the lender, all the unofficial rules that the banking system has set up now work in your favour. The borrower pays all of the fees associated with setting up the loan, including the appraisal and administration fees, and usually the legal fees."

8. Control—As the lender, you control all of the terms, the principal amount, the loan period and the interest rate.

9. Retirement income stream—You can invest your mortgages in non-RRSP loans for a retirement income stream. Then you can structure the transaction so you will receive a monthly payment from your borrower, which you can spend if you wish.

"This is a tremendous income-generating strategy for retirees and semi-retirees," said Jonquil, "because of the higher returns and lower risk involved!"

RRSP Mortgage Borrower Benefits

"There are also benefits for the borrower who is looking for $30,000, $50,000, $100,000 or more to invest in a profitable project," added Jonquil. "We'll now look at how becoming a borrower could benefit an active real estate investor saving for retirement."

1. Can complete the deal—An RRSP mortgage can get the deal done if you are an active real estate investor looking for a first mortgage on a property, but you are not able to qualify for a bank mortgage.

"Suppose the prospective property is $200,000 and you only have $50,000 as a down payment," said Jonquil. "You can't get a traditional first mortgage so you find somebody with $150,000 in their RRSP. You could approach them to put a first mortgage on your property, just as a bank would do. You buy the property with your $50,000 down payment and the $150,000 RRSP first mortgage. This represents about seventy-five per cent of the value of the property and provides excellent security for the RRSP lender."

2. Access to funds looking for better returns—With credit tightening up over the last couple of years, lenders are being more and more cautious and becoming more difficult to deal with. Private lenders that use RRSP funds represent a trillion dollar market where there is money looking for a place to get decent investment returns.

"When someone with RRSP funds understands this concept," said Jonquil, "it's amazing how much money is available!"

3. Creates a win-win—Most RRSP holders are not familiar with this strategy so you are able to create a win-win situation. You can show the lender that they can make a secure double-digit return on their money while holding good security on their investment, so their risk is low.

"Many borrowers mistakenly focus too much on the interest rate and not the entire deal as a financial transaction," warned Jonquil. "They get stuck on the high interest rate and don't do a deal that would have made them a lot of money. On the flip side, most individual investors are thrilled to get a double-digit return on their money. The opportunity to make ten per cent or twelve per cent, especially when it's a net return with no commissions, is a dream!"

4. Simple process—As a borrower, you can deal with a lender who is not going to put you through all of the hoops that a normal bank would. In general, it is much easier to work with a private lender than a traditional bank.

5. Flexibility—A lender may be willing to accept no payments for six months, so you can improve your cash flow while still getting access to capital. When you sell the property you pay the lender the principal amount, plus the balance of interest that has accrued. You can afford to pay the lender a slightly higher interest rate for their flexibility. It truly is a win-win situation.

6. Optimum cash flow—The mortgage can be structured to create optimum cash flow for the property. Since all of the terms of the mortgage are negotiable, you are able to find middle ground that gives you both what you are looking for.

7. Zero fees—There are no commissions paid to the financial industry for setting these loans up. This cuts out the middleman and allows the borrower to save money, because there are no extra fees or commissions.

8. Mortgage placement flexibility—RRSP mortgages can be provided as first, second, or third mortgages on virtually any legally registered residential or commercial property in Canada.

9. Fix-up property—Banks generally do not like lending money on a property that needs major repairs. An investor could lend RRSP money to allow you to buy that property. They may charge you twelve per cent or fifteen per cent interest, but it is only for a short period of time while you renovate and flip the property and pay off the investor. The interest you pay is minor compared to the profits you can make on the project.

10. Choice—You can use RRSPs for new purchases, or to refinance existing equity.

Deferred Payment Benefits

If you have an RRSP worth $50,000 and invest it into something that generates a monthly income, the monthly payments go back into your RRSP, so you cannot spend that money. You also cannot spend RRSP funds, because they will incur a withholding tax if funds are withdrawn.

"Let's look at an example," said Jonquil. 'You lend $50,000 from your RRSP at twelve per cent interest, which generates a monthly return of $500. After the first month you put $500 back into your RRSP. The problem is, what are you going to do with that $500? You can't withdraw it, so it will just sit in your account, as will all subsequent monthly payments. You probably can't use that money until the balance grows back into a decent amount, so getting monthly payments as an RRSP lender really doesn't have much advantage to it.

"This could be a good negotiating point with the borrower," said Jonquil, "to increase your returns." She wrote three options on the flip chart:

1. monthly payments would earn eight per cent interest
2. quarterly payments would earn ten per cent interest, and

3. one annual payment would earn fourteen per cent interest.

The modest extra interest that the borrower will pay is outweighed by the convenience of deferring the payments and helping the borrower's cash flow.

Mortgage Lender Protection

Jordan asked, "Do you have some tips for a passive investor looking to become a lender using an RRSP mortgage?"

"I sure do," said Jonquil, as she went back to the flip chart.

1. Determine lending criteria—Determine your lending criteria and stick to those criteria. If you want security and safety, then first mortgages are generally lower risk and more stable. If you are looking for a higher return, then secondary financing will normally provide higher returns.

2. Get legal support—Get a good real estate lawyer who is going to be on your side and will act for you in your transactions. Understand the process that applies in the province where you are investing.

3. Ensure protection clauses—Ensure that the mortgage is drafted by an experienced real estate lawyer and contains the clauses that you need to protect yourself. Not all real estate lawyers are familiar with arranging arm's length mortgages using registered accounts.

4. Know your market and market value—Know the market value of the property that you are lending on and the market where the property is located. Is it stable? Are indicators positive or negative? Is employment up or down? Are people moving to the area? Are job opportunities increasing? View the property and get an appraisal on the property.

5. Protect property value—Know who you are lending money to and manage the risk of them allowing, or causing the property to decline in value. Set the rules up front and make regular visits to the property.

6. Mortgage up to four years—Keep the length of the mortgage to a maximum of three to four years, especially with RRSPs. The longer the mortgage term, the higher the probability is that market values could drop.

7. Deal with problems—If a problem develops, act immediately. Do not delay over late payments, or wait and hope that the borrower is going to make good on the debt. Make it known that it is company policy to act on day one for any late payments.

"From everyone's interest," said Jonquil, "it appears that you will be thinking of how you can invest in real estate and generate better returns, since you can now get around the roadblocks of 'no time' and 'no money'.

"Next week you will learn strategies to protect the retirement savings that you generate. We will review the different asset classes and look at the big picture—the global financial economy and how it works. Your homework this week is to Google 'James Rickards' and his book, *The Death of Money.* Be ready to discuss your findings and the implications for you and your retirement savings."

Chapter 11:

PROTECT YOUR ASSETS

"The homework this week was quite different and probably foreign to most of you, wasn't it?" Jonquil surveyed. "Most people aren't aware of the bigger financial picture. Who checked out James G. Rickards, or his book?"

Again she was impressed as every hand went up. "Let's hear some of your findings and how they could impact your retirement savings," said Jonquil.

Jonathan was really into the macro-economic perspective and how global events could impact his financial future. He had already read, *The Death of Money*, as well as Rickards's previous bestseller, *Currency Wars;* he also followed Rickard's tweets @JamesGRickards on Twitter.

"I've been impressed with Rickards," said Jonathan. "Unlike many other authors of the financial-doom-and-gloom books now on the market, Rickards takes a very measured approach, based on history and empirical evidence. Even if you don't accept his conclusions, his monetary history, the history of the gold standard, and his chapters on China, Germany, the BRICS (Brazil, Russia, India, China and South Africa), and other emerging markets are well worth the read."

Rickards was trained both as a lawyer and economist, is a portfolio manager, and has been an international financial advisor to U.S. intelligence agencies and the Department of Defense.

GLOBAL EVENTS IMPACT LOCAL LIVES

"It's quite intriguing, and scary at the same time, that global events can impact our local lives!" said Jonathan. "The American dollar has been the global reserve currency since the end of the Second World War. If the dollar fails, as Rickards is predicting it will, the entire international monetary system will fail with it. There is no other currency that has the deep, liquid pools of assets to replace it."

Jeff found out that the international monetary system had collapsed three times in the past hundred years, 1914, 1939 and 1971. Each collapse was followed by an unstable period of war, civil unrest, or significant damage to the stability of the global economy.

"Rickards shows why another collapse is rapidly approaching," said Jackie, "and why, this time, the institution of money itself is at risk."

Jordan discovered that another collapse would not be unusual, but also came to realize it would not be the end of the world. The major powers will sit down and reform the system.

Jeremy, the group's U.S. citizen, jumped in, "The optimists have always said there's nothing to worry about. Confidence in the American dollar will never be shaken, no matter how high the U.S. national debt, or how dysfunctional the government. Rickards is saying the opposite," Jeremy continued. "While Washington is gridlocked and unable to make progress on long-term problems, China, Russia, and the Middle East oil-producing nations are doing everything possible to end U.S. monetary dominance."

ECONOMIC PREDICTIONS

Jonathan noted that many economists have been making the same predictions for the past several years. "Rickards has produced the best book to date," Jonathan said, "that explains why the existing order cannot continue, along with likely scenarios of how it will end. The potential results are financial warfare, deflation, hyperinflation, market collapse or chaos."

The essence of Rickards' argument is that because of the mis-management of the dollar by the Federal Reserve and recent government administrations, the dollar will lose its international standing. "By collapse of the dollar," Jonathan said, "he means the loss of confidence in the purchasing power of the dollar by both central banks and the people who use it."

This loss of confidence will likely to lead to inflation, which happened in the 1970's, and the destruction of capital, and our savings. It could result in the opposite, major deflation, which occurred in the 1930's in many parts of the world, and what Japan is experiencing today.

"Rickards explains why each scenario can occur," said Jonathan, "largely depending on the actions of the Federal Reserve. There appears to be no way out of the debt crisis for the United States. If the U.S. tips into deflation, the debt-to-GDP ratio will worsen, because there is insufficient nominal growth. If the United States tips into inflation, the debt-to-GDP ratio will worsen due to higher interest rates on U.S. debt."

Jay Googled GDP and relayed the Wikipedia definition:

> *Gross domestic product (GDP) is a monetary measure of the value of all final goods and services produced in a period (quarterly or yearly). Nominal GDP estimates are commonly used to determine the economic performance of a whole country or region, and to make international comparisons. Nominal GDP, does not reflect differences in the cost of living and the inflation rates of the countries.*
>
> *GDP is not a complete measure of economic activity. It accounts for final output, or value added at each stage of production, but not total output or total sales along the*

entire production process. It deliberately leaves out business-to-business (B2B) transactions in the early and intermediate stages of production, as well as sales of used goods.

SAVERS AND PENSIONERS SUFFER

"We will be penalized the most," warned Jonathan. "Real incomes will fall and savers and pensioners will suffer." Most nations, major banks, and multi-national companies will survive and muddle through until finance ministers and leaders put together a new set of rules. According to Rickards:

> *'If social unrest emerges before the financial elites restore the system, nations will be prepared with militarized police, armies, drones, surveillance, and executive orders to suppress discontent. The new financial system will not be based on dollars. China, Russia, oil-producing countries, and other emerging nations will collectively insist that the U.S. monetary hegemony, their political dominance and authority over other nations, will end and a new monetary standard will be created.'*

The Federal Reserve and other major central banks are trying to walk a tightrope of creating just the right amount of inflation, in order to solve the fiscal problem of too much government spending, through monetary policy.

"It's a catch-22." said Jonathan, "The more these institutions intervene in markets, the less they know about real economic conditions, and the greater their need to intervene."

Rickards spends time making a persuasive case for gold. He suggests:

> *'The United States and the IMF should lead the world to the gold-backed SDR, which would satisfy Chinese and Russian interests while leaving the United States and Europe with the leading reserve positions.'*

Jay again Googled SDR and read the definition out loud:

> *Special Drawing Right (SDR) is an international reserve asset, created by the IMF (International Monetary Fund) in 1969, to supplement its member countries' official money reserves. SDR's can be exchanged for freely usable currencies. Its value is currently based on a basket of four major currencies, the U.S. dollar, euro, Japanese yen, and pound sterling. The basket will soon be expanded to include the Chinese renminbi.*

"Of course, there is one way out," said Jonathan, "which Rickards ignores, probably because that does not look politically possible. That is for the U.S. Congress to radically cut government spending and regulations now."

Jenny was shocked to find that everyday citizens, like us, who save and invest have become guinea pigs for the central bankers, big banks and national governments that always survive by patching together new rules. The real victims of the next crisis will be small investors who assume that what worked for decades will keep working.

Judit said, "Rickards explained the difference between money and wealth. Money is transitory and may soon be worthless, if central bankers and politicians continue on their current path. True wealth is permanent and tangible and has real value worldwide."

"This is very significant," said Jonquil. "It's not too late for us to prepare."

Rickards explains the power of converting unreliable paper assets into real wealth, hard assets like physical gold, income-generating property and land, fine art and antiques, and other long-term stores of value. "How are you going to protect yourself when the international monetary system collapses?" asked Jonquil.

PAPER ASSETS

"First, let's look at 'paper assets'," said Jonquil, "and why Rickards said they are unreliable. He recommends converting them into hard assets, or real wealth, to protect and preserve your wealth."

Paper assets have three different meanings, depending on whether you are discussing business, investments, or fiat currency.

1. Fiat Currency

"We'll start with fiat currency," said Jonquil, "as this will help you to understand the predictions that James Rickards was writing about."

Jonathan immediately pulled up fiat currency in Wikipedia and paraphrased the definition for the group.

> *Fiat money is a currency established as money by government regulation, or law. The term derives from the Latin fiat ('let it be done', 'it shall be') used in the sense of an order or decree. Fiat money can be defined as:*
>
> - *Any money declared by a government to be legal tender.*
> - *State-issued money which is neither convertible by law to any other thing, nor fixed in value in terms of any objective standard.*
> - *Intrinsically valueless money used as money because of government decree.*
>
> *It differs from 'Commodity money' that is created from a good, or commodity—often a precious metal such as gold or silver, which has uses other than as a medium of exchange.*
>
> *It also differs from 'Representative money' that represents a claim on such a commodity. Gold or silver-backed*

representative money has the legal requirement that the bank of issue redeem it in fixed weights of gold or silver.

Fiat money's value is unrelated to the value of any physical good. A coin is fiat currency to the extent that its face value, the value defined by law, is greater than its market value as metal.

"Many people are shocked that the U.S. dollar is a paper asset," said Jonquil, "as are all fiat currencies in the world, except for the Swiss Franc. These paper currencies are no longer backed up by the long running gold standard. Instead, they only have value because their respective issuing governments, and their currency users, say they have value. Fiat money is used solely as a means of payment.

"The Swiss Franc is a lonely exception. The Swiss constitution requires that for every four paper or electronic currency Swiss Francs in existence, there must be one Swiss Franc worth of gold in the Swiss National Bank vaults. Since the Swiss only value their gold holdings at around $250 per ounce, and gold has been trading between $1,300 and $1,400 per ounce, the Swiss actually have a greater gold backing to their currency than the face value.

"Historically, governments would mint coins out of a physical commodity such as gold or silver, or would print paper money that could be redeemed for a set amount of physical commodity.

"Fiat money is not convertible and cannot be redeemed. Fiat money rose to prominence in the 20th century, specifically after the collapse of the Bretton Woods system in 1971, when the United States ceased to allow the conversion of the dollar into gold."

"Because fiat money is not linked to physical reserves," said Jonathan, "it risks becoming worthless due to hyper-inflation. If people lose faith in a nation's paper currency, like the U.S. dollar bill, the money will no longer hold any value. This is what Rickards is predicting."

2. Business

Where business is concerned, paper assets are assets that you cannot easily use or change into cash. They also have very low liquidity, meaning they are difficult to sell. The term in this case literally arises from assets that are valuable on paper, or that have a paper only value.

3. Investments

In investments, paper assets are pieces of paper that define ownership of an asset such as stocks, currencies, bonds, money market accounts, and similar investments. For paper assets to have a tangible value there must be a working financial system to back them up and exchange them.

Jonquil asked the group to pay close attention to the potential vulnerability of paper assets regarding investments. "If a financial system collapses," said Jonquil, "then paper assets usually sharply decline along with it. The majority of Americans, even more than Canadians, have placed an overwhelming percentage of their money in paper assets. The Financial Crisis of 2007 to 2010 showed that this makes them extremely vulnerable to economic calamities."

Paper assets stand in contrast to hard assets; hard assets have actual value in the nature of the item itself. While financial collapses can cause a setback for the value of hard assets, these types of assets almost always hold up far better than paper assets.

EVAPORATION OF PAPER WEALTH

"A confusing aspect of paper wealth is that it can increase, or decrease, across an entire economy without any changes to the real economy," said Jonquil. "This is known as 'asset price inflation or deflation'; a change in the aggregate level of prices without corresponding real change. Paper wealth does not 'come from' or 'go to' anywhere. Prices just go up or down."

Jonquil gave real life examples, "When the stock market crashed in 2000 and the real estate price bubble burst in 2008, people asked, 'Where did the money go?'

"Let's look at the pros and cons of paper assets involving investments."

Paper Asset Advantages

Very liquid—quick to get into and out of

Easy entry—not a lot of time or effort to begin investing in stocks and bonds

Cash flow—stocks that pay dividends can provide long-term cash flow

Tax advantages—profits are taxed at a lower rate

In Canada, capital gains are currently taxed at fifty per cent of the gain, and that gain is now associated with the taxpayers individual tax bracket. Dividends earn a tax credit than would generally incur less tax than interest income.

Paper Asset Disadvantages

No control—company management decides how the company makes and spends money, and manages its profits and liabilities

Volatility—stock prices can rise and fall dramatically, especially in uncertain economic times

No leverage—mutual funds, or stock shares cannot be leveraged unless you already have approved paper assets with a brokerage

High fees and commissions—charged on the majority of trades, whether you are buying or selling

SOFT ASSETS

Judit asked, "Are there soft assets and, if so, what is their role?"

Jonquil answered, "Soft assets are human resources such as people, skills and knowledge, and intangible assets like information, brands and reputation. They are hard to value and are not usually reflected in company books or inventory. The impact of soft assets is reflected in company management decisions that translate into profitability and subsequently into stock valuations in your investment portfolio."

HARD ASSETS

"Hard assets also have three different meanings, depending on whether you are discussing business, investments, or currency," Jonquil said.

1. Business

As a company manager, Jeremy was very familiar with hard assets for business.

"A hard asset is a tangible and physical item or object of worth that is owned by an individual or organization. It is the opposite of an intangible item, such as goodwill or a patent. Hard assets, for bookkeeping and accounting purposes," said Jeremy, "are listed on the left-hand side of the balance sheet. Hard or tangible assets include physical assets like land, buildings, inventory and equipment, and financial assets such as cash, credit and financial instruments."

When analysts calculate a company's intrinsic value, a portion of this underlying value is derived from the value of its hard assets. These hard assets are considered particularly valuable because they can be used to produce or purchase other goods or services.

2. Currency

"In currency transactions," said Jonquil, "hard assets are synonymous with currencies that the public generally has faith in, such as the U.S. dollar, or the euro.

3. Investments

"Rickards was referring to hard asset investments with intrinsic value or real wealth," said Jonathan, "when he compared them to paper asset investments."

Hard asset investments include gold, silver, diamonds, platinum, oil, natural gas, land, real estate and other physical holdings. Hard assets are an excellent hedge for inflation. During periods of high inflation and negative real interest rates, equities and bonds do poorly while commodity/hard assets appreciate in value.

Jordan had heard of a hedge but wanted clarification.

Google man Jay, jumped in and read the Wikipedia definition.

> *A hedge is an investment position intended to offset potential losses/gains that may be incurred by a companion investment. In simple language, a hedge is used to reduce any substantial losses/gains suffered by an individual or an organization.*
>
> *A hedge can be constructed from many types of financial instruments, including stocks, exchange-traded funds, insurance, forward contracts, swaps, options, many types of over-counter and derivative products, and futures contracts.*
>
> *Public futures markets were established in the 19th century to allow transparent, standardized, and efficient hedging of agricultural commodity prices. They have since expanded to include futures contracts for hedging the values of energy, precious metals, foreign currency, and interest rate fluctuations.*

Jonathan explained that Rickards' hedge comment referred to hard assets rising in value with inflation, compared to paper assets, where their value is eroded by inflation. This provides protection for the owners of hard assets.

In general, hard assets are negatively correlated to both stocks and bonds. In other words, when stocks and bonds decline, commodities tend to appreciate. As an example, from 1970 to 1981, the S&P 500 total return was only 20% over eleven years, compared to an 1100% increase in oil prices and 550% increase in Western Canada farmland prices during the same period.

Jackie asked, "What is S&P 500 and what is its significance?"

Jay, again, was ready and paraphrased the Wikipedia definition:

> *The Standard & Poor's 500, often abbreviated as the S&P 500, or just 'the S&P', is an American stock market index based on 500 large companies having common stock listed on the NYSE (New York Stock Exchange) or NASDAQ. It is one of the most commonly followed equity indices, and many consider it one of the best representations of the U.S. stock market, and a bell-wether, or leading trend indicator, for the U.S. economy.*

Jonathan anticipated the next question and paraphrased the definition of NASDAQ from Wikipedia:

> *In 1972, NASDAQ stood for National Association of Securities Dealers Automated Quotations. Now called the NASDAQ Stock Market, commonly known as the NASDAQ, it is an American stock exchange and is the second-largest exchange in the world by market capitalization, behind only the New York Stock Exchange. The exchange platform is owned and operated by The NASDAQ OMX Group.*

Gold

Jonathan then talked about gold as a hard asset for asset protection. Gold has been regarded as valuable for 2,600 years. Anyone who already has money wants to secure and protect it, so they are learning about gold, 'the secret of the wealthy.'

"For security, capital protection and a hedge for inflation and deflation," said Jonathan, "Rickards recommends converting a small percentage of your assets (ten to fifteen percent), into physical gold. Monetary gold bullion can't go bust and can never be worthless. Physical gold, such as monetary gold bars, is the best way of securing value when everything 'goes down the drain'."

Gold is a form of currency and is accepted in 194 countries. Gold bullion in small units is the best insurance if something unexpected happens in our lives and can easily be exchanged for goods and services, which is impossible with large units.

Jonathan shared his top reasons to buy gold:

1. Gold offers protection against inflation, deflation and currency reform.
2. Gold is a stable investment in crisis times.
3. Gold is a limited resource and is not reproducible.
4. Gold bars are global cash.
5. Global demand for gold is higher than supply.
6. Purchase and sale of investment gold is exempt from tax in some countries. In Canada, paper gold and silver are taxed as investment income. Physical bullion is taxed as a capital gain.

He showed a graph on his iPad as he explained, "Global unrest has triggered renewed interest in gold as can be seen from this chart from 1995 to 2016. Gold has recently seen its best start to the year since 1974. Exchange-traded funds (ETF's) that track gold have surged in popularity."

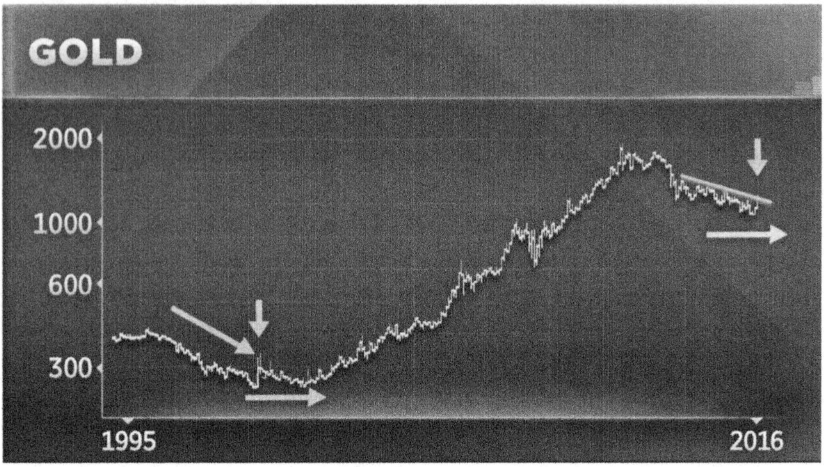

Rickards prefers physical gold, the hard asset, compared to paper assets like ETF's, for better protection from a major financial meltdown or an online 'zombie attack', either of which could severely impact investors.

Jay knew what a zombie attack was and paraphrased the Wikipedia definition for the group:

> *In computer science, a zombie is a computer connected to the Internet that has been compromised by a hacker, computer virus, or trojan horse and can be used to perform malicious tasks under remote direction. Botnets of zombie computers are often used to spread e-mail spam and launch denial-of-service attacks. Most owners of zombie computers are unaware that their system is being used in this way. Since the owner tends to be unaware, these computers are metaphorically compared to zombies.*

"The single biggest knock against gold," said Jonathan, "is the fact that gold doesn't yield anything. However, in a period where cash doesn't yield anything either, gold looks very attractive. Most people don't know how to buy gold, especially in small units."

Jonathan went on to tell the group about a unique online system he found that allows anyone to purchase gold bullion in small affordable units, including one gram gold bars, specialty gold cards and gold collector cards in limited editions. Automatic monthly withdrawals can be set up as a savings and security plan.

Jonquil jumped in and told the group that she had a friend who was successfully using this online system to buy gold as an investment and as gifts for family and friends. She said, "You can learn more at **theretirementcrisis.com, Online Tool #11**."

Real Estate Versus Paper Assets

Jonquil appreciated Jonathan sharing his knowledge of gold with the group. Now, she wanted to compare another hard asset—real estate—to paper assets.

1. Borrowing Leverage—You can put down $40,000 to buy a $200,000 investment property and get $160,000 from the bank. You now own assets worth $200,000. If you put $40,000 into paper assets, you only get $40,000 worth of assets.

2. Appreciation Leverage—If the value of your $200,000 property increases by five per cent in one year, which is below average for many areas, you are $10,000 richer.

"The best part of this story," said Jonquil, "is that even though eighty per cent of the money to buy your property came from the bank, you don't have to give them eighty per cent of that $10,000. It's all yours! If your $40,000 paper asset increases by five per cent in a year, you're only $2,000 richer."

3. OPM—The bank could loan you a lot of money to buy property, even millions, to buy an apartment building, or commercial building. That is using OPM (Other People's Money) at its best! You can also go to mortgage agents and hard-money lenders, if necessary. The bank, mortgage agents or hard-money lenders will not loan you a dime to invest in paper assets. You will have to use your own money to buy paper assets, unless you already have approved paper assets with a brokerage and they agree to loan funds on margin.

4. Full Replacement Insurance—You can insure your property for its full replacement value against loss. You cannot insure paper assets against any type of loss.

5. Control—You have no control over the real estate market. However, you have control over the 'value' of your property. You can increase value by doing minor improvements, major renovations, and keeping full occupancy. You have no control over the stock market, or the management of your paper investment. There is nothing you can do to increase the value of your paper assets.

6. Joint Ventures—You can form joint ventures with many investors, family, friends and associates. Together you can buy or invest in big properties that will yield remarkable returns.

Jonquil painted this picture of going to your family and friends and saying, "Let's pool our $50,000 together so we can buy a bunch of shares of 'Future Company' or some 'green start-up'."

7. Tax Advantages—Depreciation and expenses can be used to reduce the income from your real estate investments. If you have one or more investment properties, and travel to inspect your properties or to other locations to look for properties to invest in, your travel expenses are a tax deduction.

Jonquil said jokingly, "Try to do that with paper assets!"

Jonathan pointed out that in Canada, there are very specific rules regarding expenses for real estate investors and suggested reviewing the CRA rules online.

Jonquil promised to add the CRA link to her website: **theretirementcrisis.com** for the group to reference, under **Online Tool #12**.

8. Cash Flow—Properties generate cash flow, which is money in your pocket every month. Most paper assets do not provide cash flow, unless a mutual fund pays monthly dividends.

9. Real—You can drive by and see your investment. You can live in it, paint it, add an extension beside it, a patio behind it, or plant a tree in front of it. It's real! Paper assets are just pieces of paper.

10. Homes for People—Investing in real estate provides shelter and homes for people. You can give people with past credit problems a chance to own a home or live in a safe neighbourhood.

"It's a great feeling!" said Jonathan. "You don't get that feeling from calling a broker and buying a bunch of stocks."

PROFESSIONAL PROTECTION

Legal Support

Part of protecting your assets is receiving knowledgeable and experienced legal advice. This is especially true when you are investing in real estate.

"You now know that there are many avenues for investing in real estate," continued Jonquil, "single-family homes, multi-family apartments, student rentals, long term hold, rent-to-own, fix and flip, and passive, semi-active and active investing, to name a few.

"Agreements and contracts need to protect all parties involved. For instance, joint venture agreements must be specific regarding responsibilities, commitments and 'what-if' scenarios. Rent-to-own agreements must specify option payments, credit repair commitments, time period and 'what-if' scenarios. It is the responsibility of all parties to seek legal advice."

"Active real estate investing is a business and needs to be operated that way," said Jonathan. "Business structure can play a large part in protecting assets and also reducing taxes. As a real estate investor, review your options with a knowledgeable accountant and have an experienced real estate lawyer draw up the papers for the chosen structure.

"Any one of us can have unexpected legal issues arise. When you are an active real estate investor, legal questions and issues can appear almost every day. Your identity could be compromised and prevent you from obtaining credit; your driver's licence could be suspended; or worse, you could land in jail for a crime you didn't commit."

"Do any of you have up-to-date wills to protect your assets?" Jonquil asked.

Only three hands went up.

"What about powers-of-attorney?" Jonquil continued.

One hand went up.

"If you have a business, having an estate plan that links with your will can protect your assets from being clawed away from your spouse and children."

Nobody in the group was aware of the importance of these tools to protect their assets.

"Some people don't have a lawyer, or don't know a lawyer," Jonquil pointed out. "Most don't want to pay, or can't afford to pay for a lawyer. But I found a service where anyone can access legal protection and everyone can afford it. From real estate to document review to will preparation, lawyers are on call to advise you with any legal matter, no matter how traumatic or how trivial it may seem.

"You can learn more about this service at **theretirement-crisis.com, Online Tool #13**."

ACCOUNTING SUPPORT

Another key aspect of protecting your assets is receiving knowledgeable and experienced accounting advice. As an active or full-time real estate investor, you can use your tax savings for further investments.

Jonathan mentioned again that active real estate investing should be operated as a business. Protecting assets and reducing taxes can be facilitated with the proper business structure. An experienced and knowledgeable real estate accountant can be invaluable when reviewing your options.

Whether you decide to be an active, passive or somewhere in between real estate investor, ensure that you have knowledgeable professionals on your team that you enjoy working with. Life is too short to 'endure' working with an 'expert' that makes you feel uncomfortable, or beneath them.

"You want someone who is competent at what they do, but you also want someone with a certain degree of humour!" said Jonquil.

"I totally agree," said Jonathan.

Jonquil had done her due diligence and provided a tremendous amount of information over the last three months for the group to digest. She warned them that she was not licensed to sell anything and all of the information was strictly for their learning.

"Please utilize the online tools and information on my website: **theretirementcrisis.com**. Also ensure that you do your own due diligence and thoroughly research whatever strategies you decide to act upon. Consult an accountant, lawyer or advisor that is knowledgeable and experienced in that specific area."

Jonquil concluded the meeting, as usual, with some homework. "We've learned and shared much together," she said. "However, all the knowledge in the world won't help you improve your retirement situation unless you take action. That is next week's topic. Please share a quote or story that you use to motivate yourself into action. If you don't have one, find one that moves you."

Chapter 12:

TAKE ACTION

"This is a bittersweet occasion," Jonquil said. "We've been meeting at the same place, at the same time, every week for three months and this is our last meeting in person together. We've learned much together and had some fun along the way."

Jonquil challenged the group to think about these questions:

- What is your biggest wish, your lifelong dream, and what is keeping you from going after it?
- Are you waiting for 'everything in your life to be right', to 'have all your ducks in a row'?

That will not happen. You will never 'have it all together'. That's like trying to eat 'once and for all', clean the house 'once and for all', or fill up the car 'once and for all'.

TAKE ACTION

She then asked the group members to share a story or quote that moved them about taking action.

Jackie started with a quote from Sinara Stull O'Donnell,

'You don't get the part if you don't audition.
You won't get the job unless you apply.
You won't get organized unless you try.
You won't clean your closet unless you start.
So start!'

Jordan quoted Jack James,

'Be empowered. The way to get confidence is to be confident.
Believe in yourself, and others will believe in you too.'

Judit lived by this quote from Mary Englebreit,

'Worrying does not empty tomorrow of its troubles.
It empties today of its strength.'

Jay found a quote from Bob Urichuck,

'ACTION—this is where the magic begins.
You have to become action-oriented. You need a "do-it-now" attitude.
The first two letters of goals are "go." NOW is the time to get going.
Do not tell the world what you can do—SHOW IT!'

Jonathan read this quote by Robert J. Ringer that keeps him motivated every day,

'Action today! Develop the habit of living in the present. The best day really is today, so get started now, no matter what your problems are and no matter how long you've already procrastinated.'

Jeremy quoted Paulo Coelho, *'Close some doors, simply because they no longer lead somewhere.'*

Jeff surprised the group with his powerful story and forewarned them, "Please, don't wait, or your story might sound like this one:

"On Wednesday, December 3, 2003, I walked into Margarita Pizza to buy one of their award-winning traditional Italian pizzas. They were the best in the city in 1999. I've been stopping there for the same reason every other week for the last 30-some years. But there was something different there that day. For the first time ever, Attilio, the owner, was not behind the counter.

"A friendly woman informed me that she and her husband had just acquired the business a few days earlier. After owning the business for forty years, 76-year-old Attilio Janiello finally decided to sell it and enjoy the fruits of his labour. And from what I heard, the 'fruit' was very large.

"The deal was signed and money changed hands on the previous Friday at four o'clock in the afternoon. His friend told me that on the way home from the bank that afternoon, Attilio stopped at a travel agency to enquire about plane tickets for a trip to Italy that he was planning to make in the coming months.

"On Tuesday, about eight o'clock in the morning, while having breakfast with his wife and reading his 'Corriere Italiano', Attilio died of a heart attack. He enjoyed the fruits of forty years of labour for less than a hundred hours.

"I heard since that he was ready to take that trip about fifteen years earlier. He was ready, but he didn't go. Perhaps he was waiting for the time to be 'just right'. He waited too long."

Jenny followed with another powerful story that put more tears in many eyes in the room. "Alexa Whitehorse is a native girl. My Dad first met her when she was twelve years old. It was about ten o'clock on a frigid, February Friday night when he pulled into her village. As he drove to a friend's cabin, he noticed a young girl figure-skating in the 'hockey' rink. It was way too cold for the boys to be out playing, so the rink was empty, except for Alexa.

"She was very good at it. And she loved it. Everybody was urging her to continue and become a professional skater. She skated until she was sixteen, winning local competitions and a regional championship, but she slowed down, and eventually stopped. She let go of her dream. She told a friend she was waiting for 'everything in her life to be right' before pursuing her dream again. After graduation, she went to work at a local store as a clerk.

"On January 4, 1993, a car accident on the road near her village left her paralyzed from the waist down—twenty years old, a beautiful, vibrant young woman, in a wheelchair. It brought tears to his eyes when he first saw her again.

"Now in her forties, she's adapted to her new life. But she told him she often dreams of a genie coming to her in the middle of the night to offer her one wish. 'I'd give anything for one more chance to lace up my skates that pinched my toes when I put on extra socks. I'd give anything for one more night out on the rink, all to myself, with the numbing wind, the bumpy ice, the scratchy PA system playing the song I used to skate my choreography to, 'Someday my prince will come' . . . I'd give everything for that privilege, even the rest of my life'.

"Alexa Whitehorse's biggest dream is to be able to skate again one day," said Jenny. "Don't wait! One day you might regret it."

Jonquil told the group, "Here's the best recipe I know for getting rid of procrastination.

> *'DOn't waIT! DO IT.*
>
> *Every single day. Even if it's just a little thing like making a phone call, reading an article, conversing on social media, talking to a friend. At least ONE thing, EVERY day, that takes you closer to your DREAM'."*

Jonquil quoted Shaw who said,

> *'People are always blaming their circumstances for what they are. I don't believe in circumstances. The people who get on in this world are the people who get up and look for the circumstances they want, and if they can't find them, they make them.'*

She continued, "Everyone has problems and challenges and circumstances and crap to deal with every day. We know that our education system fails miserably at equipping us with the initial skills we need to be successful in our financial lives. My hope is that our meetings have helped you to understand 'the system' and how you really can create a prosperous retirement for yourself and your family, by just doing simple things consistently.

"We learned strategies that provide a unique combination of simplicity, attractive returns and risk minimization that most people have never heard of. Your next step is to take action."

PLAN TO SUCCEED

Taking action starts with planning and setting goals. Studies show that less than ten per cent of people set goals and less than five per cent achieve their goals.

Tony Robbins said, *'Setting goals is the first step in turning the invisible into the visible.'*

"I'll end this meeting by reviewing seven common barriers to achieving your goals, and specific ways to overcome them," said Jonquil. "Please take notes and be honest with yourself. What barriers do you need to get over or around, and when will you take action to work on them?"

1. Lack of Commitment

Action speaks louder than words. Even though people say they want to achieve certain goals, their actions show they are not committed to their objectives. Because of this lack of commitment, they do not give goal attainment their full effort. As with anything in life, if you do not give it your all, you only get mediocre results. Setting and pursuing goals takes time and commitment.

Be Determined and Persistent

Set goals in writing and regularly review them by measuring and managing your progress toward your objectives. Be stubbornly determined and persistent, but also be patient. Your determination and patience will be strong enough to overcome any setbacks or delays that are thrown at you. Never give up. Seek opportunity in adversity and view every closed door as a positive step in a better direction. Pablo Picasso was profound when he said, *'Action is the foundational key to all success.'*

2. Failing to Plan

Failing to plan is planning to fail. Many people set well-defined and realistic goals as a great first step. However, they skip the next crucial step, which is to build a plan. They take action and jump into buying investments without ever making a plan. Their attention to planning, or lack thereof, is directly related to achieving, or not achieving, the results they want.

Adopt a Thorough Plan

Understand the importance of planning. Think about the words that management expert Alan Lakein said, *'Planning is bringing the future into the present so you can do something about it now.'*

3. Analysis Paralysis

Many people let questions and doubts paralyze them. They think they cannot start on a goal until they have all the answers to every possible scenario. This is a self-defeating approach to goal setting. No matter how long and how hard you prepare, you will never have all the answers to your questions.

Be Analytical and Selective

Focus your analytical efforts on two scenarios: the worst case and the best case. Be very selective and careful where, why, and how you invest any of your resources. Do not deplete your resources by pursuing random opportunities that do not align with your overall objectives. Some people may think you are reluctant. However, in reality, you are being selective. You cannot be pushed into emotional decisions based on fear or greed. When an opportunity matches your criteria and takes you closer to your goals, you act quickly. Martin Luther King, Jr. wisely said this, *'You don't have to see the whole staircase, just take the first step.'*

4. Fear of Failure

Most people are afraid of failure and that fear keeps them from setting meaningful goals. This attitude turns failure into a self-fulfilling prophecy.

Research and Be Comfortable with Calculated Risk

When you plan for success, you are not afraid to fail. Thoroughly research potential risks before making a commitment and plan accordingly. Take calculated risks and be open to new opportunities and ideas.

"If you protect the downside," said Jonquil, "the upside will take care of itself".

When you are comfortable with risk, and when you believe in yourself, others will believe in you also. Henry Ford often said, *'If you say you can't, you're right! If you say you can, you're right!'*

5. Fear of Success

The other side of the coin is fear of succeeding. People are reluctant to set or pursue meaningful goals, because they worry that people will envy them or think negatively of them. Many also fear that others will anticipate their eventual failure, which is one more thing to avoid!

Seek Personal Growth

Be committed to multi-dimensional growth, not just financial growth. Continue to educate yourself and surround yourself with like-minded people who encourage success. Listen to CD's, watch YouTube videos, or read a variety of self-improvement books to improve yourself. You will be more focused on what you will become in achieving your goals, rather than on what others have accomplished or how they may judge you. You want the destination, because it is a planned and meaningful goal. You also need to enjoy the journey! Victor E. Frankl once observed, *'When we are no longer able to change a situation, we are challenged to change ourselves.'*

6. Feeling Unworthy

Many people sabotage themselves because they do not feel they are worthy of attaining their goals. They do this without even realizing it. Perhaps, they suddenly walk away from an opportunity that could really move them forward, or they shy away from building key relationships. Feeling unworthy is usually the result of a lack of self-confidence.

Express Confidence and Worthiness

Research demonstrates that you can fake it until you feel it and be it! Confidence can be acquired by practicing the use of strong body language, through education, meaningful goal setting and a real world understanding of calculated risk. Quiet confidence is the foundation of goal attainment. Your personal ego is not the driver. You make investment decisions because you are confident in your ability to produce a high rate of return. You share your stories to help others, not to make you feel good about what you have accomplished. Dale Carnegie gave this advice, *'If you want to be enthusiastic—act enthusiastic.'*

7. Lack of Focus

Some people set goals, but set too many. By failing to direct their focus, many people are being unproductive. They wander their way through life, never mastering anything in particular, and never understanding or acknowledging their personal responsibility for their lack of direction.

Maintain Focus

Goals are said to be the energy source that powers our lives and can be used to channel and concentrate our energy toward what we desire. Realize that you can produce positive outcomes by focusing on one goal at a time. Maintaining focus gets more difficult as you expand your business or investment portfolio. You can manage this by building a team around you to support your weaknesses; that allows you to focus on your areas of brilliance.

This keeps you engaged and when you are engaged, you are focused! Alexander Graham Bell had this memorable advice, *'Concentrate all your thoughts upon the work at hand. The sun's rays do not burn until brought to a focus.'*

Jonquil noticed that everyone in the group took notes and captured each profound quote on paper, iPad or smartphone to refer to whenever they needed support.

"Please remember two more quotes," Jonquil said encouragingly, "Diana Scharf Hunt said concisely, *'Goals are dreams with deadlines,'* while Larry Winget advised, *'You don't have to be good to start, but you have to start to be good.'* "

"I also have two more tools for you," Jonquil smiled. "They are powerful video clips to motivate you. Have a look at **theretirementcrisis.com, Online Tool #14** and **Online Tool #15**.

Jonquil continued, "Review your 'why' regularly as that will keep you focused and motivated. Continually picture it in your mind. Design what you want your retirement to look like, and make every investment decision with that in mind. Take action. Surround yourself with great support, and revise your goals as you grow and evolve.

Jonquil brought the meeting to a close by reviewing the three key questions each member of the group needed to figure out for their successful retirement:

1. How much do you need to save for retirement?
2. How do you invest that money?
3. How do you withdraw that money so you do not outlive your assets?

"By now," Jonquil continued, "I hope that each of you have answered questions one and three, and are developing a plan to answer question two. I know we will all take action in one way or another. Some of us will become passive real estate investors.

Others may choose to become active real estate investors. We will all take steps to preserve our wealth and prevent a retirement crisis in our lives.

"Things will go wrong. You will make mistakes. But you do not have to fear those mistakes. We only fail when we quit. Everything else is learning. Some learning is more painful than others—the loss of a spouse, friend, job, business or financial loss.

"Real estate is likely the best long-term wealth creator and, over time, it can offer you enormous financial and time freedom. It requires perseverance, patience and consistency. You just have to keep working at it. Nothing will happen if you don't take action. If you are stuck, it is amazing what shows up when you just start moving forward. Usually the missing piece is action. You will succeed if you keep going. The only way to fail is if you quit.

"There is never a 'perfect time'. Most people want to wait until the perfect moment to take a leap, whether into real estate or some other venture. Remember the 'Don't Wait' stories from Jeff and Jenny," said Jonquil, "and enjoy the ride on your road to retirement!

"Your homework for next week, or more appropriately, when you are ready to take action, is to review and utilize the online tools at **theretirementcrisis.com**. I put them all there on one handy website, because I have found these tools to be very helpful.

"Let's keep in touch and share our successes online! Perhaps, we could reconvene once or twice a year to share our stories, strategies and successes. I wish the best of luck (and investment practices) to all of you."

ABOUT THE AUTHOR

A life-long learner and entrepreneur, Bob McNaughton believes that you can generate wealth from real estate even if you have no time, knowledge, or available cash. Having experience in corporate management, marketing, project management, and in establishing his own business, Dog & Pony Productions Inc., Bob puts his writing, communications and leadership abilities to use in educating those looking to invest wisely.

Bob invested in the stock market and mutual funds for thirty years, with some degree of success. However, times changed, and the minimal control over wildly fluctuating markets and low interest rates lead Bob back into real estate where he had started in his early twenties. Bob aligned himself with mentors who had developed successful systems and he built a dynamic real estate investment team. He and his team specialize in rent-to-own (RTO) properties—helping people with financial difficulties qualify for a mortgage and achieve the dream of owning their own home. He also helps investors who are looking for better returns, but lack the knowledge and experience or face time constraints, and guides them to financial success.

His first book, *The Retirement Crisis . . . and The Real Estate Solution,* is a natural extension of his desire to educate and empower others. In stimulating storybook fashion, Bob created a fictional group of people to present his incredible knowledge, life lessons and investment experience, so anyone can learn and utilize his powerful ideas to avoid a retirement crisis.

Bob is happy to help anyone wanting to take action and set themselves up for a successful life and a fulfilling retirement. He can be reached at:

bob@**theretirementcrisis.com** or
theretirementcrisis.com

Bob and his wife live in St. Thomas, Ontario with their cats and chocolate labradoodle dog, Truffles.

Made in the USA
Monee, IL
04 November 2026

67385373R00115